Diana Love Story (PT. 3-4)

Graduation, and we plan to be a part of the season.

Tina Scott

Before I even went to the toilet, I got up and called Diana. She wanted to come to my place, and I told her to come over after 1:30, so I could rest, clean up, and get back to normal. After we finished talking, I went to the bathroom to shave and wash. When I was done, I felt ready to rejoin my kin. Camilla was at a friend's home, which was fortunate because it made it possible to speak to my parents without her there. When I told them about how bad things had been with Adrienne, they were really helpful, acknowledging that Ade had misbehaved. I was hoping it wouldn't jeopardize their relationship with Marvin and Sandy.

Then I mentioned the other issue that was worrying me. "Diana is at a sleepaway party like she does every season. It means we'd just see each other once a week, on her day off, assuming I would get the same day off. She asked if I wanted to work there for the summer, and although it sounds amazing, there are some drawbacks. First, I wouldn't see you and Camilla all summer, and then I'd just have about five days off before starting classes. Second, I'll earn somewhat less revenue, at least a thousand dollars less. And I promised Sy and Marilyn (the print shop owners) that I will work all summer to fund their holidays. I'm at a loss about what to do. Diana will be here at 1:30 to discuss this, and I'm at a loss for words."

My parents both reached for one of my palms, and that small touch conveyed a lot of affection and encouragement to me. I'd always been willing to speak to them and bring some problems to them. I was very fortunate because I met some of my peers who hardly spoke to their parents at all. My father talked on their behalf. "Forget about your promise to Sy and Marilyn, Jon. Don't even think about sharing time with us. Do you believe that not having Diana will be detrimental to your relationship? I'm talking around seeing her once a week or less."

"It couldn't be useful for it. Yet, I trust her in the same way she trusted me with Adrienne. She won't end up in a summer romance, and neither will I."

"And so you'll spend much of your spare time at school together, right? But it's summertime. I understand that eight weeks would seem like a long period. But if you believe you can do it, let her go. However, if you are compelled to spend the whole summer with her, go to work with her. We'll figure out the capital. We will assist you."

"No way, no how. You're always doing enough for me. And now that you're sick, you can preserve your resources anywhere you can."

That time, she responded. "Jon, a thousand dollars isn't going to make a difference in our lives. You are our baby, and we will do all in our power to assist you. I believe you can hold your promise to your boss. They've been kind to you over the past two years. But you must still do what is right for you, and only you know what it is."

It was entirely my choice. They weren't going to make that for me, which was the proper course of action. Diana and I had to work things out together. My parents, on the other hand, offer me, sound counsel.

Diana arrived on schedule, and after greeting my friends, we went upstairs to my room to chat privately. I just had to leave the door slightly ajar. It's your parent's home, and you have to follow your parent's laws.

I was the first to talk. "You did believe me last night, didn't you, honey? Were you concerned that I would not be loyal to you until I called?"

"No, it does not. No, not at all. I knew I could depend on you. I wasn't concerned in the least."

"That's how it is for me. I'm not worried that you'll find someone at camp who would break it up with me. And I'm not looking to find anybody here. What I mean is, Diana, I told my employers I'd be there this summer. They're relying on me. I would love to work at camp if it weren't for that, my vow to them. So it isn't really about wealth. I made a promise. Still, before we reach a definitive decision, let me ask you a question: Do you believe our friendship is good enough to be separated for the majority of the Summer?"

"Yes, I do. I'm not going to get entangled with anybody at camp, and I'm sure you won't either. So I'll miss you if I go. I'll miss my relatives more than anything else." Diana cradled me in her embrace and kissed me many times. "I adore you to the moon and beyond. It'll be difficult to be without you for the majority of the summer."

"The same thing happened to me. But after the summer is through, we'll have too much time to look forward to. We'll be together for the rest of the year. I don't say any of the time. We just need one cooperative, or mainly absent... roommate, and we'll spend so much time together that we'll learn to despise each other!" With a wide smile, I said.

"Never, ever! You're quite the character, last night proposing marriage and today discussing hating each other. For some couples, that equates to ten years." We embraced for a moment, rocking back and forth. We couldn't do much more with my parents in the kitchen. "Are you sure, Jon? If you like, I'll do something else for the summer, like the YMCA's day camp (the YM-YWHA). I realize we'll be fine in the end, but I don't want to be separated for too long." Her mouth teased mine as her hand rubbed across my jaw.

"I'm not going to tell you what you can do, honey. I can tell you that if you go, I'll miss you terribly. Yet I care so much for you that I trust you to do what's right for you. If you want to go to Surprise Lake (her camp), I suggest you go for it. It's not even that long, an hour and a half either way?"

"Yes, on the east side of the Hudson, just north of West Point. You'll pay us a call whenever you can?"

"You couldn't keep me safe, honey. As long as I can have the same days off each week, I'll be there every week. Please, darling, do this. I want you to do what brings you joy."

"If I did it right now, your parents would kick me out," Diana said with a lustful embrace. "Seriously, are you sure? I'd be leaving eight days after we graduated."

"Diana, hurry up!" With a grin, I said. "Consider how unique any time we see each other. We could only get a hotel room and shack up for the day."

"That is ideal! I wish we were alone right now just thinking about it." Several more kisses.

"That's nice because they'll be going grocery shopping shortly. Let's head downstairs for a few minutes. We should be able to be along shortly."

"Camilla, how are you? I don't want her to come home too soon."

"She'll be at a birthday party before 4 p.m. We'll have plenty of time if my parents left in the next hour."

While my mother was getting ready, we went downstairs and sat with my father. She was the sort of lady who never left the house without her makeup on. "You never know who you're going to meet," she used to say.

My father wanted me to assist him with everything in the garage, which was his code for speaking to me alone. He talked to me when we arrived. "I'm not going to advise you to 'behave' when we're out, Jon. I'm fairly sure I'm smarter than that. But keep in mind that your sister will be arriving home around 4 p.m. You must be presentable before she arrives. Also, please open your browser. I don't want the same thing to happen again."

It was a little embarrassing to speak about this openly with him, but I admired his honesty. "Dad, we'll be...respectful. I guarantee it. That's about what I have to think about it."

I went back inside, and he waited in the car for Mom. They were on their way to the store in five minutes, and Diana and I returned to my space after a respectful period.

"Did your father mention something to you in the garage?" she inquired. "However, I'm fairly certain I can guess the general subject."

"Are you sure you want to know?" She agreed with a smile. "He's fairly sure we're going to be together now, but no particulars have been provided, and he reminded me that Cammy will be home around 4 p.m. and that we should be, and I quote, 'presentable' by then. Sorry, you were curious."

Diana was flushed in the chest. "I think I knew they knew about us, like my parents, but it's always strange knowing they know...you know?" We both smiled as we kissed each other.

"I understand. I also realize Cammy will be home in a little more than an hour. Before then, I want to make sure my girlfriend is fully satisfied. I am overjoyed."

"Whatever we do, you make me happy, really happy. In your bed, your home, a gallery, or while dancing with you. I've never been happier in my life." Her wide brown eyes shone brightly. Then, teasingly, she unbuttoned her short-sleeved blouse, and I studied her, never moving my gaze away from her. She then reached behind her, and her bra fell loose, which she threw on the concrete. Diana licked her fingertips on both palms, closed her eyes, and sighed as she traced them across her areolas, allowing the moisture to shine through the lovely pink rings.

"Are you sure?" Diana said in a lustful whisper. Her eyes were just halfway wide. "If you like, you can prove it to me. In truth, I am adamant. Let me see how difficult you are for me, kid."

I got up in front of Diana, who was sitting on the edge of my bunk. I unbuttoned my jeans while she continued to play with her breasts, flicking them with her nails every few seconds, making her scream. Diana noticed how ready I was about her as I took off my denim cutoff shorts and briefs. I was fully stiff, all six inches of my groin and its gentle upward curve. "MMMMM," she moaned, then bent over and licked all over me, head and shaft, and it was my turn to moan.

"You're a naughty, naughty kid," I yelled as loudly as I could. "You should always get spanked for being such a poor kid."

"I believe you need some restraint, young lady. Get up and remove your pantyhose."
"We'll make it do more than a tingle, but first..." Diana leaned slightly over, reached under her short blacktop, and steadily pushed her panties down her thighs. I was almost drooling as I watched her. She understood how to make me laugh. She was getting pretty good at it.
Diana sat on my lap, her sweet, round butt poking up in the air just enough for her to feel me on her tummy but not so far that she pressed down so tightly on me. I took my right hand and stroked her lower back, as well as the curve of her ass, and then down the back of her thighs. Diana was mewing, noises of joy and contentment that I broke by tightly pressing my hand against her right side, a sharp cracking sound that took her off balance.

"Oh, no! That hurt, sir!" She screamed, but she didn't try to flee. I was certain that I had not struck her too strongly.

"Don't complain, otherwise things would be much harder for you," I warned her.

Diana whimpered as she wiggled around on my knee, "Yes, sir." She gasped out again but didn't protest after another somewhat rough slap on her left eye. Her cheeks were both peach and seemed attractive. I repeated my pattern, slapping each cheek twice more, and Diana's moisture oozed onto my leg. "Please, Sir, I've had plenty. I'm going to be a nice kid. I guarantee it!"

"It's not looking positive right now. It's okay to be a bit naughty."

"Sir, indeed! I'll prove to you how naughty I'm always capable of being!" Diana sprang on her feet, took off her top, rolled me onto my back, and assisted me in swinging my legs until I was on my bed in the right direction.

Still, I couldn't say her because my mouth was preoccupied with kissing her lips and then her clit. Her reddish cheeks shimmied just in front of my eyes as I pounced on her most delicate spots, which I had memorized by that time. She was still worked up, so I got a little trickle of her delicious juices that saturated my cheeks and jaw.

Diana said with a wicked grin, "Who is being mischievous this time? I will have to spank you the next time we get together. Just not right now. I'm way too hot for you." She got down to her knees and knelt, her head resting on a cushion.

"You're a bad kid," I exclaimed with mind-numbing delight. "And I wouldn't alter a thing about you for the universe. Keep being naughty for me!"

Diana exclaimed, "My pleasure, boy." "You must be my evil, sexy guy."

We finally calmed down, and after exchanging more kisses, I realized the time was nearly 3:30. I informed Diana we had to get washed up and downstairs by 4, so we dashed to my bathroom and took a short shower. Ten minutes in the bathroom, ten minutes drying and grooming (Diana used a shower cap to keep her hair dry), and ten minutes getting ready and straightening out my bunk. To freshen the weather, I sprinkled some space freshener around. When we dressed appropriately, we went downstairs to get something to drink before putting on some music as though it were some other day.

Cammy returned home some 15 minutes later, overjoyed to see Diana. Cammy embraced both of us and told us about her friend's birthday party. Then she went upstairs to transform into more comfortable clothing, and my parents arrived when she was out. Diana and I assisted them with the bags, and mom welcomed her to dinner.

That night, we brought Cammy to play mini-golf and then ice cream. We became the epitome of a young couple in love. Cammy didn't even look at Diana and me as we kissed. She was thrilled to see us in that state.

I went to Diana's the next day for a while, and we spoke once more until she signed her contract and mailed it. She was finally leaving for the summer. We'd be apart for most of July and August. We were hoping that as a couple, we'd be confident enough to pull it together. Just time will say.

Diana and I didn't have as much 'fun' time together as we would have wanted or as much as we were accustomed to during the next four weeks. Exams had to be taken, and final articles had to be published. We entered an informal discussion group of around 15 people who met a couple of afternoons a week to exchange ideas and generally support each other. Back then (and still today), New York State was the only state requiring Regents exams in various topics. You didn't have to take any subject. Still, you had to take English and Social Studies, a foreign language, and a three-course category of science or math (algebra, geometry, trigonometry, or genetics, chemistry, physics, and earth science) with a specific form of degree. I'm not sure why this was important. But it was true. The best thing was that Diana developed some friendly contacts even though it was late in the year.

Diana has previously completed both of her Regents and took all AP courses and graduate-level classes to gain college credits. I was taking two AP courses, English and History, when she was taking five. Overall, my girl was brilliant. So, with all of the learning and my internship, we just had Friday nights to have fun. Often it was just a bite to eat and a movie; on other occasions, it was a function to attend, and we always had time to indulge our sexual lives, but not as much as we had been used to.

Seniors' exams were finally completed on Friday, June 15th. The 19th was the date set for graduation. The Friday night was a big gathering, not entirely legal, but everyone who wanted to participate chipped in to get four kegs, which we schlepped to an NYC public park, off the parking lot, where there was a lot of drinking and music. Several joints were moved about. I restricted myself to two beers....well, two and a half....because I was driving, but Diana went a bit crazy, something she rarely did before and got pretty wasted. She wasn't inebriated, but she was fairly buzzed by midnight.

Diana wrapped her arms around my neck and replied, more loudly than she usually did in public, "Hello there, sweetheart. If you want to take me anywhere and take me hard?"

A few people nearby laughed loudly as they saw her. This was a version of Diana that no one in our class has ever seen. It was just a matter of time before word got out.

"You seem to be a little blasted, honey. I believe we can go get you some coffee before I drive you home." I didn't want to exploit her partner or not. Besides, Diana wasn't looking her best at the time.

"Honey, I guess we should wake you up a bit. After that, we'll be able to work out the lot. Come on, my darling." I pulled her to my vehicle, sat her in her seat, and fastened her seatbelt. I got in my car and drove to yet another diner (there were dozens of them throughout Queens back then, all owned by Greek-Americans, like it was a law or something). Diana noticed where we were as I pulled into the parking lot and said in a moaning voice I'd never heard from her before, "Hello there! I assumed we were going to get married!" I couldn't stop myself from laughing uncontrollably. It was way too amusing. "What are you laughing about?" she mumbled. It took some time for me to recover from my laughter. Diana didn't get what was so amusing. "What are you laughing at, Jon?" she inquired.

"Please accept my apologies. You're only really amusing right now. Let's go inside for a coffee and toast." When we got there, I made sure she had two cups of coffee and a toasted bagel. I drank tea and ate a bagel. We didn't say much; we took our time and let time and coffee do the talking. Diana was sobering up for only an hour and a half, but she wasn't doing much healthier. "I can't believe I got so drunk," she admitted, her face paler than normal. "It's like death has frozen over."

"I've been there a couple of times. I'm not a major drinker, which could come in handy when we get to work. Smoking marijuana, on the other hand...safer, that's in my opinion. You don't feel ill from it, nor do you get a sickening hangover from it."

"Yeah, I'm sure it's fantastic, but it's illegal. If you are caught, your life could be tainted by a criminal record. It should not be unconstitutional, in my opinion; however, it is. Anyway, thanks for looking after me and not using me for love, sweetheart. I'd have hated it as I sobered up, so I thank you for not taking advantage of my drunkenness."

"You weren't in a situation to make an informed choice, honey. I respect you so much to hurt you like that. In the next two weeks, we'll have plenty of time for intimacy. Following that...."

"No, not too many. My next cycle isn't expected until the first week of July, at the very least. I'd like to see you as soon as possible before I go. Just not tonight, "She said, weakly nodding.

"You've struck a bargain. Are you happy to go home, in your opinion? Can you believe you're sober enough?"

"Jon, you are right. Please get me home. And once more, thank you. Another excuse to adore you." She held my hand in hers. I charged the bill, and we got in the car to drive around.

Diana said when we arrived at her house, "You don't mind if I don't want to make love to you tonight? I despise saying no to you."

"Diana, please don't ever sound as though I'm putting pressure on you. And let me know if you feel it. There will still be other nights and days. I'm excellent. It's fine if you can't kiss me goodnight. I realize you're feeling under the weather."

"More than a bit," she attempted to grin. "I suppose it's not that horrible. I don't believe I'll get ill. Jon, thank you for being so kind to me. I adore you to the moon and beyond." She reached in and embraced me tightly. Except for a quick peck, there were no kisses.

"You get your shut-eye, honey. You're focusing on your speech for tomorrow, aren't you?"

"True. Salutatorian is a salutatorian. It's a big deal."

"Hey, it's kind of a huge deal. That day in the hall, when I first saw how lovely you are, I told you that so many of us wish we had your intelligence and would love to be delivering that speech. You should be pleased with yourself. Your families will be pleased with you. Except for Will and Walt." That made us all laugh; they'd be very proud of their sister. "Don't forget that I'll be proud of you," I promise my heart would burst with pride. Not to mention my parents and Camilla. "In particular, Cammy."

Diana gripped me ever more tightly. "I wish I didn't have to quit you or that I could welcome you in for the night." "I'd like to wear you all night."

18

"I wish we could as well." Tomorrow night, we'll head back."

"Or we might hang at home." My parents are heading out tomorrow night, and Will and Walt will almost definitely head out for a few hours. Please contact me in the afternoon of tomorrow. "I adore you, Jon."

"I adore you, Diana." "Thank you very much."

We kissed goodnight, and I led her to the entrance, making sure she wasn't wobbly. I went home, missing her after she went inside. I snuck out a pair of panties she had sent me before going to bed and jerked off furiously, thinking about my sweet, gorgeous, and brilliant queen. Cumming wasn't quite as enjoyable as Diana's, but it was everything I had that night. Thinking of her was such a big turn-on. I hid her underwear once more before turning over and falling asleep.

XXXXXXXXXXXXXXXXXXXXXXXXXXXXXXXXXXXXXXXXXX
XXXXXXXXXXXXXXXXXXXXXXXXXXXXXXXXXXXXXXXXXX
XXXXXXXXXXXXXXXXXXX

After I got home from work (tired as hell!) and before I went to bed for a two-hour sleep, we spoke after I got home from work. It was necessary if I was to spend the evening with Diana without falling asleep on her. With a literal sense. I may have dozed off as we were making love; that's how tired I was. I awoke at 6:30 a.m., showered, dressed, and spent some time with my dad.

"What are your plans for tonight?" Cammy inquired, the brightest, brattiest grin on her face. I believe she was hoping to accompany us if we headed out anywhere.

"I'm sorry, Kiddo, but we're all hanging out tonight," I swear we'll take you out one night before Diana leaves for the summer. And you'll see her at the graduation ceremony on Tuesday." They were eating, and I was starving, so Diana and I took Chinese food for dinner. Mom's potted chicken, on the other hand, smelled delicious.....

"In truth," my mother chimed in, "would you mind watching your sister next Saturday?" We're going to spend the day at Sandy and Marvin's house. You wouldn't be willing to accompany us?" She sent me a similar glance.

"I don't see how Mom." The only explanation I'd go will be if Adrienne is there because we're not talking right now. We may be finished as partners."

"What happened between you and Adrienne, Jon?" Camilla inquired. My father was aware of the problem, and I thought he informed my mother, but Cammy...well, I couldn't describe it to a 12-year-old.

"I'm sorry, Cammy, but it's not anything I can discuss with you. It's more appropriate for adults."

"Does it have anything to do with sex?" My precocious sister blurted out, and I was relieved that I wasn't feeding or I might have swallowed on something. I shouldn't have been surprised; my sister was almost as smart as Diana. She was also very wise.

"Camilla Rose!" my mother exclaimed emphatically. "It is not a question you should be asking your buddy!" His personal life is his own, and besides, if you want to know something about sex, just ask me! And then I'll know whether or not to inform you!"

Cammy seemed to be angry. She didn't do something bad at all. She was getting closer to maturity, and she was intrigued. However, some things became much too intimate, particularly between an older brother and his younger sister. "Cammy, Adrienne, and I fought," I said softly. The reasons are really specific, but it was a poor battle, and I'm not sure whether we can mend things between us. I'm hoping we will because I'm missing her. I suppose only time can tell. Still, I can't tell you much about it."

Cammy seemed to recognize it, even though she wasn't thrilled with it. I assured my parents that I would take care of her. Diana and I will spend the day doing things with her. It was then time for me to head to Diana's.

Camilla approached me as I approached my front entrance, just as I was about to leave. "Who is Jon?" I apologize if I asked you a question that I shouldn't have. "I have no idea."

I knelt to eye level, which needed less and less bending all the time. She was getting higher and higher every day. "No, you have no idea. But there's plenty to be sorry for. I'll gladly answer most of your questions. That's why you have a big brother. But there are certain topics I just cannot discuss. Maybe when we're older. MUCH older. "Like when we're in our sixties." She burst out laughing and embraced me.

"Hi, Diana!" she screamed as she dashed up the stairs to her place.

"I'll do it!" I chased her down and went to Diana's. Five minutes later, I was kissed on the mouth by my best lips in the whole universe. In full view of her relatives. She was making up for the night before when I didn't get a goodnight kiss.

"Hello, sweetheart," Diana said quietly, kissing her gently. "Do you miss me?"

"Throughout the day. "Seeing you helps relieve the agony," I said, smiling.

We went to her family's living room and stayed for ten or fifteen minutes, often talking to her parents, before the twins left for a friend's house after their father ordered them to be home by ten o'clock. Diana informed me that she had already arranged for dinner and that it will be delivered shortly. The benefit of having a partner who understands you too well is that she knows what to order for dinner without having to think.

Dinner arrived ten minutes later, and her parents left a few minutes later. We were alone, enjoying dinner and looking forward to more alone time. "How did you sleep the night before?" I inquired as we ate a chicken and shrimp dish with potatoes.

"I fell asleep as soon as I placed my head on the couch, but I was up at 6 a.m., peeing and feeling nauseated." I got some water and drank it slowly, and by 7 p.m., I felt much stronger. Then I slept until ten o'clock and felt good."

"You're fortunate. Any citizens may have been sick the whole day. Except for graduation, you should feel relieved that school is done. "You made a bit of a scene last night," I said with a wide grin.

"How come?" "What did I say or do?" Diana inquired, alarmed.

"You mentioned bringing you somewhere and taking you roughly. It's very loud. I'm talking about LOUD. Then I said that we wanted to get some coffee.

Diana came to a halt in the midst of swallowing whatever was in her mouth. She became as white as a wall. "No, I didn't."

"All right, you didn't. And that you did. "I swear to God."

"Oh my goodness! I'm not going to the graduation ceremony on Tuesday! I'm not going to expose my face in front of those strangers!"

"Of course you will. It would humanize you in the eyes of all who believe you're some kind of arrogant genius. "You, like the majority of us, are a human being." I was on the brink of laughter when I smiled.

24

"I'm happy you find this amusing. "How come you didn't stop me?"

"I couldn't put an end to you. I have no clue what you were trying to suggest because you were shattered. After that, I got you out of there. Still, people saw you. Don't worry about it. You'll joke with them about it at our tenth anniversary."

Diana didn't understand the joke. She was doing a gradual burn when she threw away the paper plates and put the leftovers in the fridge. I approached her from behind, wrapping my arms around her tummy and kissing the side of her cheek. Diana tried to resist me at first, but when I kissed her cheek to the side of her mouth, then the back of her neck and shoulders, Diana's icy cold attitude melted away, and she soon turned to face me, returning my kisses with all her desire. Her arms were wrapped around my waist, and her lips were kissing mine. Then she kissed the side of my neck and the back of my throat, and I was listening to her advances.

"You remember, sweetheart, I never got to be my king's serving wench. Why don't you take me upstairs, my King, and do whatever you want with me? "I can be accommodating."

"Affordable? "Let's see how accommodating you are," I said as I picked her up and lifted her the stairs to her bedroom over my back. Diana burst out laughing as she bounced along with my steps.

"It's Jon!" "Please, put me down!" She burst out laughing, her earlier anger forgotten. "I've just eaten!" "You're going to make me puke all over your ass!"

"Then you'd best not vomit!" Vomiting on the King is a capital offense!" I threw her on her bunk, and she burst out laughing like she was Cammy's age.

"Sire, did I offend you in some way?" "Did I say anything to irritate you?"

"Not at all, my wench. We've already agreed we have to have you. And have you we shall," I said commandingly as I began removing my top and undoing my trousers. "So, baby, what are you waiting for?" "Take off your clothes for your King!"

I screamed like I pretended to be rain.

"Indeed, my King. And accept my apologies for the wait." Diana hurriedly changed out of her clothing. Her skin tone was pinkish, and her desire was visible all over her body. My curiosity was visible through my body when my shorts were off. The head was reddish, on the verge of turning black. Diana licked her lips unintentionally.

"Please come here, child, and serve your King." "Don't you know what to do?"

"I think so, my Lord." If not, I'll find something out." Diana was on all fours in front of me, her mouth moist and needed, while I stood by the side of her bunk.

"Yes, my wench, that is fantastic. "Just wonderful," I said, again and again, urging Diana to use her oratory skills to bring me great joy. She moved back to my balls but not using her fingertips. As I looked along her back, I noticed the great curves of her hips narrowing until flaring high from the width of her fantastic butt. I kept asking how I had overlooked her sexiness and elegance all those years.

I could scent her, sweet, beautiful, feminine, filling the space, yet as horny as she must have been, she stayed in character, completely submissive. Yet I couldn't make her that helpless. She stared up at me, puzzled. "Did I offend you, my King?"
"No way, my poor daughter. I just want to try you out as well."
We both laughed; the vocabulary was, to put it mildly, florid. But it was entertaining and a little kinky, and we were having a good

time playing the game. "Stay just where you are; don't shift." Then I broke character and kissed her many times, receiving a huge smile in exchange.

I stepped behind her and climbed into the bunk, placing my palms on her cheeks and softly and lovingly touching her while I began to lick her butt all over. Maybe a true king might not have bothered to be so loving, but I wasn't a true king. "That feels so wonderful, my King," Diana said with a long, deep sigh. "You might claim it at any moment."

Diana moaned and shuddered as I took my first bite, and when I licked and kissed her gash and lips more vigorously, her lower body rolled about a little more wildly, and the groans I heard drove me to devour her delicious slit.

"My lovely lady. You're incredibly tight. "I sighed. "You're fantastic."

"Thank you so much, King. You're in a great mood." I began thrusting, gently at first, bending over her and kissing the back of her neck, causing Diana to shiver all over. She giggled a lustful laugh that fueled my need for her even further. We spoke less as I went quicker, so we could just appreciate our sexual gratification. I had a layer of sweat on my neck, and the smell was blending with Diana's feminine scent. "Harder yet, my King," she grumbled. "Please fuck me some more!"

"As you wish, my love," I said, quickening my pace. It was a beautiful experience any moment Diana and I was together, whether we were acting like two depraved sex maniacs or being as caring and tender as possible. This time, it was unmistakably the former. Wicked, filthy, and a lot of fun. I offered her a light spanking, and she yelped gleefully from the surprise and sting.

My climax did not sneak up on me; rather, it erupted from inside me. My balls drew tighter to my body and twitched like Diana, and I let go of my seed inside her. My hips continued to pump, churning our milk into foam. Diana slid forward softly, and I drifted with her, nestling her smooth butt into my lap. We were exhaling heavily when Diana said quietly, "Thank you so much, my sexy King. You're too kind ", and we all laughed. Diana stretched catlike before reaching back over her head to caress the back of my neck and arm, and I nuzzled her neck and shoulder.

Brow. My hands sought her breasts and curves, and she sighed as I moaned as she sighed.

"You're too much fun," I said next to her ear, causing her to turn her head back towards me. "It's even sexy."

"You're just a lot of fun, sweetheart. And you are welcome to be my King at any time. "Diana said this as she turned to kiss my lips. "Pretty much at any moment."

When I remembered to remind her, we cuddled for a bit. "I almost forgot about it. I informed my parents that Camilla would be taken care of the next Saturday. They'll be out all day and into the evening."

"Not a challenge. We'll find something enjoyable to do. Just bear in mind that this is our last weekend together until I go. Staff must be present the next Thursday for four days of orientation, even though they have already served there. But this is our last Saturday night together for the next two months." Diana will be away for more than eight weeks; it was beginning to set in. If our schedules aligned, I'd see her once a week. I squeezed her as much as I could without harming her.

I changed the topic and asked, "What else is there to say? Our families will gather at graduation on Tuesday."

"You know, I didn't even consider it. Is there anything to be concerned about?"

"I can't believe so," I replied. "Maybe we should all head out to lunch after that. I'll tell my parents about it tomorrow."

"I'll do the same thing. Why am I concerned about the prospect? "She inquired of me.

"I'm not sure. I'm in the same boat, so there shouldn't be any problems." Even the concept was strange.

We woke up, washed up, and then straightened her room before getting ready before her brothers arrived home. She took the notes for her Salutatorian speech downstairs and read them to me, asking for feedback on some points, wording, and principles. I sent her some suggestions, some of which she approved and some of which she refused. It didn't bother me; it was her voice, and it had to sound and feel right to her. Will and Walt arrived home about 20 minutes late, just when Diana began to worry, but she vowed not to warn her parents about their tardiness. They sat with us, and by that time, they had warmed up to me. They weren't as close to me as Cammy was to Diana, but we got along well.

We went out to find something to drink when her parents got in. After the night before, it was strictly something soft, but we went to another tiny local club with live music and danced for a couple of hours, some quick hits but more when things slowed down, in between enjoying a couple of club sodas. We shuffled on the tile, Diana's head turned sideways on my chest, her head coming straight to my lips for an easy kiss. It was fine after our previous activity and enjoying each other.

I brought her home at 2:30 and went home after several kisses—Goodnight at her entrance. We took Walt, Will, and Camilla to the Mets game the next day. We sat way up in the $1.50 cheap seats (1979, remember?) and had a wonderful time, with my parents paying for hot dogs and Cokes. Cammy, who isn't a major baseball enthusiast, was well-behaved and got along with Diana's brothers. It was just an enjoyable afternoon that seemed completely normal. When I dropped Diana and the boys off at home, we asked her parents if we should have lunch with my dad, and they agreed it seemed like a nice idea. When I got home, my parents liked the concept and said it was time to meet her relatives.

On Monday, we each did our own thing; I played softball with colleagues, and then a group of us got haircuts (every barber and hair salon was packed that day!) Diana and her mother went shopping for camp uniforms. At 10 a.m. on Tuesday, we graduated from Queens College's auditorium. I got up, showered, washed, and dressed up in my finest suit and tie. Since I was anxious, I missed breakfast and instead drank some juice. My family was all dressed up, including Cammy, who was wearing a bikini. She stood next to me in the living room as we waited for our parents and said, "I'm so proud of you, Jon," and gave me a huge hug. I was taken aback and shed a little tear when I embraced her back.

"Thank you, Cammy. You that I'm proud of you as well. I'm grateful you're my niece. And though you might be a jerk at times." She giggled when I looked down at her. So to say, the other lady of my world.

We left early enough for me to stop at the florist to get mom yellow roses to thank her for being my mom, and I got Camilla a single white rose because she was my sister, and I didn't want to miss her out. They were all moved, and my father gave me a pleased look. We arrived at graduation at 9:30 a.m., half an hour early. I drifted about, greeting different friends until coming across Diana and her family. We exchanged soft kisses, me in my red cap and gown and Diana in her white ensemble. We crossed over to where my family was waiting and introduced ourselves. Diana burst into tears when I handed her the dozen red roses I had gotten for her from my father. "Dammit, Jon, now my makeup is going to be a shambles!" In front of our parents and the senior class, she embraced and kissed me. "I am so going to make this up to you tonight!" she said in my ear. Of course, more photographs were made, of Diana and me together, of all of us with our respective families, and we also had someone taking a photo of everybody all together. We felt like a large extended family.

We stood next to each other (we both had "G" last names, Glazer and Grossman) and locked fingers when the ceremony began. Then she was called up to give her address, and I sat there, perhaps almost as proud as her parents, as she gave a fantastic 10-minute speech. As she sat down again with me, I couldn't save myself from embracing her in front of everybody, and we were greeted with cheers and catcalls. After Elizabeth finished her address, we took turns receiving our diplomas by the last name, and everybody flipped their tassels to indicate that we were finally graduates. The students exchanged handshakes and cheek kisses. It was almost done. The next chapter in our lives was about to start.

Our parents got along well at lunch, which was at a busy Italian restaurant where my parents had invited them all over for a little barbeque on Sunday. That night, though, there was a huge party at a nearby bar that the class had rented out with a DJ, and it was a lot of fun. Diana and I stayed mostly sober (neither of us wanted to replay the previous week), but it didn't stop us from having a wonderful time, chatting and joking with friends, and dancing the night away.

My friend Mike came over, a little tipsy, and said, "I'm delighted for you! You two make such a cute pair!" He was slurring his thoughts, and I was relieved that he lived two blocks away and could walk alone. We laughed when we thanked him, but I was concerned about the people who drove there and the amount of alcohol we consumed. Diana and I discussed it, and we gathered about a half-dozen sober people to volunteer as a driving service for our classmates who were too intoxicated to drive. Starting at 1 a.m., we took turns filling up our vehicles for everyone that wanted a lift, driving them around, and then returning. It took two to three drives for each of us to drive everybody safely, but we managed it, and there were no injuries that night.

It was after 2 p.m. before we finished, and as much as Diana and I decided to 'celebrate' alone, we were still exhausted. The day began 18 hours earlier. Diana turned to me in my car alone and asked, "Sweetheart, would you mind only driving me home now?" "I guess I'm too tired to pump."
We exchanged a grin, and I said, "You took the words straight out of my mouth." We'll think something up tomorrow. Maybe we'll splurge on space and spend some time together."
"I'll take care of it." You've been so kind to me. Those roses were the most beautiful present I've ever had, much better than the neckless my parents gave me for my 18th birthday. My boyfriend sent me my first flowers. "You lavish me with gifts."

"Come on, honey," I say. The flowers were much superior to the neckless. It's lovely." It was a thin gold chain with a Jewish star on it and tiny diamonds at each of the six ends.

"However, the flowers were such a nice treat, and they said too much of where your heart is." You're a great boyfriend and a wonderful guy."

We were huddled in the front seat of my car, in front of her building. Kissing and cuddling We were exhausted, but we wanted some intimate time to kiss and chat. After about ten minutes, I said, "I have to go, honey." Either that or I'm going to sleep here. You're in your room. "Along with YOU."

"As laid-back as my parents are, I don't think they'd go for it, particularly with my brothers at home." So, just go, and drive cautiously home? "Make a promise to me."

"I swear to you. In five minutes, I'll be alone. I'll contact you at noon. Perhaps a bit later. Honey, I adore you. "Thank you for a wonderful day."

"No, thank you so much, my darling. You added a personal touch to this. We'll make up for lost time tomorrow. You should depend on it."

On the way home, I had a little panic. I couldn't hold my eyes open and nearly drove into a parking vehicle, but I jolted awake just in time. That jolted me awake long enough for me to get home and into bed. Diana was the one thing I was lacking. I would have given almost anything to be able to snuggle with her in bed.

XXXXXXXXXXXXXXXXXXXXXXXXXXXXXXXXXXXXXXXXXXX
XXXXXXXXXXXXXXXXXXXXXXXXXXXXXXXXXXXXXXXXXXX
XXXXXX

On Wednesday, I had to go to work. I was still working part-time, but I worked a couple more hours than normal, from 12 to 5. I dashed home, hopped into a hot shower (I sweated profusely in the print shop, particularly during the summer), and was ready to go by 6 a.m. I told my parents that I would be arriving home late. Camilla asked if I could drop her off at her friend Wendy's place, and even though it was a little out of the way, I said yes. And if it was a half-hour detour, I might have done it. Whatever it takes for Cammy.

I dropped her off at her friend's house and arrived at Diana's a little late. She didn't mind; she was the most laid-back lady I'd ever seen. "Hi, sweetheart," she said as she slipped into my embrace in her home's foyer. We were affectionate in public by this time, including with her or my relatives. Everyone thought we were madly in love with each other. And her brothers had avoided making fun of us. "I had forgotten you. And I'm hungry! I purposefully missed lunch so that we could have a large meal. What about cacciatore chicken? "Would this be our first date?" Diana's eyes were filled with hunger, and not just for food.

I returned her smile. "Chicken cacciatore looks delicious. And dinner will be served later?"

"Enjoyed at least twice." Let's get going before I pass out from starvation!"

We spoke and kept hands while we weren't dining at Marco's, where we had our first date (we also had the same table). We had our carafe of house wine. We'd only been a couple, a loving couple, for a little over three months at the time, but we seemed like we'd known each other for years. Technically, we had known each other for years, but we didn't KNOW each other for the majority of the period, and as I reflected on it, I hated every day that had passed. It inspired me to see that we have as bright a future as possible for as long as possible. Diana and I were meant to be together, and I was fairly confident she thought the same way.

After dinner, we returned to the Holiday Inn, where we had slept on prom night. Diana was in my lap, and we kissed a couple of times. "We'll have lots of time together tonight," I said, gently rubbing my nose against hers. "Honey, I want to love you tonight." "I want to have fun with you and make you have fun with me."

"If that's what you want, then that's what I want," she said softly, her heart full of affection for me. It made me shiver, not from cold or fear, but a position of overwhelming affection. As we stood there embracing, we each undressed. We took our tops off first, no hurry. Diana breathed in my mouth, gripping the back of my head with her palms, her fingertips running through my hair, while I massaged her breasts in her bra. Her touch was full of lust, and the more she touched me, the more it piqued my interest.

"Jon, you know what that does to me," Diana said as I nibbled at the side of her mouth. You are making me crazy! "Please help me get out of my bra!" Still, I was moving slowly, teasing her, and she enjoyed it while still feeling annoyed. She grew a little forceful with me when I drew the tip of my finger down the line where her breast met her bra, both breasts. My 5'3" 105lb girlfriend was pushing her 6' 180lb boyfriend back up to the bed before the back of my legs reached the mattress, and I fell backward, with her jumping on top of me. "Jon, I need you tonight and every night if we can figure things out." I don't care if you want me to be as good as chocolate or as filthy as mud. It hurts my heart to think about leaving you next week. So I'd like to spend as much time as possible with you. Sweetheart, I adore you. Over and beyond everything." Diana's eyes welled up with tears, and she collapsed into my side, sobbing uncontrollably.

I stroked her hair and burst into tears as well. She perfectly articulated everything I was doing, my worries, wishes, and everything in between. I wasn't crying as much as she did, but this was a stressful case. We couldn't get a space every night for the next week, so we had to make do with alone time every night, in my car or at either of our houses. Even only sharing intimacy, carrying, touching, and chatting is enough. Our other desires took precedence over sex, but sex was going to be a part of that night. We just needed to get over the current feelings that were gnawing at both of us.

"We'll try our best, honey. Let's take - day as it comes, okay? We've got tonight, as Bob Seger tells. We'll think about tomorrow; he doesn't mention it. Let's only handle - day as it comes."

Diana sniffed out her eyes and simply nodded along with me. We kissed as a romantic couple; then our kisses became hotter and more passionate. It didn't take long until we were lovingly undressing each other and kissing all over our bodies. We were soon down to our shorts, me in black briefs and Diana in a rainbow pair of cotton panties. She knelt over me, her groin only a few centimeters from my face, slowly and sexily rubbing herself. She flicked her nipples with her fingers before allowing her hands to drift down her tummy to the elastic of her pantyhose. Then she slipped only the first few knuckles of her fingertips under the band and grinned down at me, as aroused as she had been before. "I need your assistance, Jon. "You wouldn't refuse me, would you?" she joked.

"I considered it," I joked. "But you're too attractive to pass up." Diana chuckled when I flipped her over on her back and pinned her upper arms to the bed. I'd met a foe I could defeat.

"Mmmmm, someone's feeling frisky," Diana said softly and seductively. "You are free to do whatever you want to me tonight, sweetheart." I am entirely yours. "I'm still completely yours." I bent in and kissed her passionately while clutching her upper arms. She didn't exactly want to flee. "So, major fella, what do you intend to do to me?"

"I hope you're still hungry," I said, a horny smile on my face. I went up to her body, my legs then trapping her arms back, just the thin cotton of my briefs keeping her arms in place. Her eyes were glassy, and she licked her lips on purpose, which was very naughty.

"Take a look at who's spoken. I could taste every single part of you. But then, a bit bit about me."

"I'm delighted." She looked up at me with wet, caring eyes as I pressed my head between her lush lips. I bent over her like a pushup, gently feeding her my nipples in and out as her tongue did incredible stuff to me. As I shifted my legs to loosen her wrists, her hands caught my a$$, spurring me on. Then she spanked me with her right hand, a strong hard blow, making me yelp when she did it again, way more than I have ever spanked her. I didn't mind because it made me so hot, and I fucked her mouth with long strokes.

I was physically and metaphorically swept away by the wicked, beautiful care she offered me. The only drawback was that I realized I'd have to find a way to handle her equally well.

As I regained my breath, I went down her body and kissed her, cum on her face and everything. It got all over us, turning us into a messy, creamy heap.

"You're incredible, my darling, so good, attractive, and naughty all at once." "I'm so in love with you," I said between kisses and body caresses.

"It was an honor, sweetheart. I'm in love with you as well, and I'd do something with you...or to you," she smirked. "I really can't believe you don't get scared when you get your cum in your mouth or on your forehead." "I thought guys despised that."

"I'm not sure about the other guys; it never comes up in discussion," I said, and we all chuckled. It was such a pleasure to laugh with her. I kissed her once more. "Wait a minute, sugar. I'll find a wet towel for us to clean up with. Then I avenge myself."

"Excellent! I can hardly wait! Jon, I'm crazy about you!" When I entered the tiny toilet, she called after me. I took a towel, immersed it in hot water, wrung it as dry as I could, and carried it into the bedroom to rid her face of my semen. Then she took the towel and did the same for me, so both of our faces were washed. We threw the towel to the ground, stood up facing each other, and kissed repeatedly.

"How can I now satisfy my lovely lady?" I inquired, trailing my fingertips over her upper breast.

"That's fantastic. But I want more. You've had me all high and bothered. You should reciprocate. "She expressed her optimism.

"Whatever you want, my darling. I'm here to make you happy."

"That's just what I was hoping you'd think." Diana embraced me quickly before falling to her knees. I could see a little moist patch in the groin, and there was a slight hint of her lovely scent in the breeze. It attracted me to her like honey to a bear. I moved my hands effortlessly around her buttocks before kissing her all over the back of her thighs and her cheeks. Diana frowned and shifted her weight slightly, tempting me to put my face in there. "Jon, you're making me sticky. You're the most wonderful lover!"

"In comparison to whom?" I made fun of her. She smiled and opened her legs wider for me. I took the cue and licked the crotch of her trousers, which were warm and damp from her natural lubrication. My nose was pressed against her snout while I licked harder and harder before Diana whimpered. I may taste her and push my lips to hers, but I couldn't ever suck on her or the pearl of her clit like that. I drew her pantyhose down over her a$$ and left them around the center of her thighs. She could only stretch her legs too far, but that was more than enough for me. Dripping juice and exuding a magnificent fragrance reminiscent of her exclusive perfume, I couldn't get enough of it.

"You're such a sweetheart, baby. I adore how much you adore me. "She spoke quietly, touching her boobs with one hand and supporting her body with the other. She continued to press back into my face, hopping about and fucking my lips. I snatched her long mane in my right hand, pulling her head back and forcing her to push out her tits. Diana appeared after I pressed my thumb against her clit. Her muscles continued to squeeze my fingertips, and her anus winked open and closed.

When Diana had had enough, I let go, slipping my fingers free and kissing her up her neck, sending her one more shiver of gratification. I flipped us on our sides and spooned her, which was one of our favorite things to do anytime we had the room to stretch out. She leaned forward and kissed my chin and cheek. "Jon, sing to me. I like it when you do."

"I'm at a loss about what to sing for you, honey." I wasn't at ease performing in front of everyone, not even Diana.

"I'm looking for something soft and pretty." So, because I couldn't think of anything better, I sang 'Ripple,' one of the Grateful Dead's sweeter tracks. Diana's eyes widened as she was positively shocked. When I was done, she said, "You did an excellent job on that! That's a great album. I had no idea you were a fan of the Grateful Dead."

"I'd think the same thing for you. We're all discovering new stuff about each other." Diana giggled quietly as I kissed her cheek. "Unfortunately, you would be absent. They'll be at Radio City in mid-July."

"I'd see if I could take another day that week. If I had a compelling excuse."

"They'll be there for three nights. I realize they aren't all sold out. I'll bring you tickets tomorrow so you can let them know when you arrive for orientation." It was a fantastic concept, but it reminded us of our impending breakup. "I've only seen them twice. Have you noticed some of them?"

"No, the only concert I've ever attended was Billy Joel's last year. I believe our whole class went to one of those series."

"Except for me. I'm not a fan of his."

"Are you serious? The whole city of New York adores Billy Joel!"

"Except for me, once again. I dislike him."

"Oh, I can't believe it! You realize you're mad, don't you?"

"That's what I've been advised. Do you think it's worthwhile for us to have our first war over this?" I greeted her passionately and sensuously. Diana and I were both able to go.

"No, I'm not interested in fighting. Sweetheart, I want to love you. I adore you as well."

That was an invitation I couldn't refuse. We kissed and touched more passionately, and in only a few minutes, I was good and hard, and Diana was equally prepared. My shoulders crossed mine, and my profile was just a few centimeters from hers. Diana's warm fingertips brushed my cheek, and I kissed and sucked them into my mouth. "My sexy man," she murmured as I pushed tighter, her clit on my pubic bone. She exclaimed, her eyes wide open, as an orgasm swept across her body. As our lips parted, I took deep breaths and said, "Honey, I adore you. My sweet love. Angel, my lovely."

Diana was crying again, except this time they were cries of affection. "Gentle Bear, you are really attractive. So cute and attractive." As a result, our pet names were born, names that lasted a long time. Yes, I'm revealing everything, but Diana became my Angel that night, and I became her Bear, or Gentle Bear when we were alone.

I thrust harder and deeper, taking Diana to another climax, and then we switched places, with her on top of me. She mounted me again slowly, then ground her butt in tight circles on my hips with her hands on my stomach. Soon after, she began to move harder, her lovely butt growing and dropping, though I couldn't see it. But I understood what it felt like to the smallest detail, including a tiny birthmark on her left eye. She was bouncing, riding me to a throbbing orgasm, so it was my turn a minute or two later.

"My Gentle Bear, I adore you. Too much to tell."

"My Angel, I adore you as well. These titles appeal to me. I particularly enjoy being your Bear. Your Serene Bear."

"It is appropriate for you. You're big and cuddly and soft, and you're so gentle." Diana kissed my chest and throat, her body glowing and wet.

"And Angel is perfect for you. You are the greatest thing that has ever happened to me. You're as though you were delivered from heaven to me."

"Jon, you're stupid and mushy right now. Yet I like it. You're such a sweetheart. It's no surprise you were a bad wrestler." We both burst out laughing. The way she mentioned it was adorable.

"Are you not tough enough?"

"No way. Yet I adore you just as you are, tender and perfect." We kissed many times more. Again and again. We only had a couple of hours, and whether we made love again or not, we should spend the time enjoying each other. And that is just what we did. We laid in bed together for the next two hours, becoming romantic—touches, smiles, and the like, as well as general chit-chat. We exchanged our secrets, which I won't reveal here, but they were stuff that made us together than we were before. And then, at 12:30 p.m., we made love in the tub, with hot water cascading down our legs. It contributed to the warm feelings we were experiencing, and when we were finished, we clung to each other like coils of thread. It was the ideal way to end our evening.

We dressed silently, climbed into my seat, and I took Diana home. We kissed each other for a long time after we arrived, sometime before 2 p.m. "Angel, I wish we could spend the night together. Every night "I expressed my displeasure at the prospect of returning home to different beds.

"I understand, my Gentle Bear. Every morning, I wish I could wake up next to you. Maybe we'll be able to move together off-campus next year. And though it seems like a long time from now."

"Yes, it is. It seems like an eternity. Let's get this summer over with, honey. I believe we're going a bit nuts."

"I understand. It's insane. Yet I know my heart longs for you all the time."

We kissed her goodbye at her entrance, as we always did, and compelled ourselves to come to a halt and call it a night. As I got home and into bed, I thought, not for the first time, how we would get through the summer apart. Despite the time, sleep took a long time to arrive.

I operated for the next two days (still part-time; Sy and Marilyn agreed to let me resume full-time when Diana left on Thursday). They were decent people.) And I spent that night and every day off with Diana. Most evenings, we had intercourse or mutual love, which was equally rewarding. Just as rewarding, to be sure. Saturday, my parents went to Adrienne's parents' home, and Diana and I brought Camilla to Jones Beach for the day; then, after cleaning and showering at my house, we took her to her favorite burger joint dinner.

Cammy began to feel ill as we were dining. She went to the shower, and Diana checked on her because she had been away for a long time. They'd all been away for a bit, and I was starting to panic when Diana returned.

"How is Cammy doing?" I inquired, apprehensive at the time.

"She'll be perfect," Diana said, a small grin on her face. She lowered her voice and spoke to me in hushed tones. "She received her first period. I offered her a napkin because she was sad and didn't have food. She needed to be quiet for a few moments. I recall how unsettling the first time might be. She was aware of what was going on, and your mother had thoroughly demonstrated it to her. Nonetheless..... Could you please do me a favor? I don't think about it. She's a little embarrassed."

"Without a doubt. I will never make her feel uneasy. My younger sister is maturing. Thank you for being there for her, Angel. I'm not sure what I might have done if it had just been me and her here."

"It isn't a challenge. I'm happy I was able to assist her." Cammy then returned to the table, appearing a little agitated. I simply asked whether she was well, and she simply nodded her head. We got out of there as soon as I could get the check and brought her home to rest. Diana accompanied her to ensure her safety before joining me in the living room.

"She's well. It was only a bit difficult for her. The first time will be a painful experience. She'll be fine. I'll inform your mother when they return home." I kissed her passionately, thankful not just that she was there with me, but she was particularly there for Cammy. My parents arrived home about an hour later, and Diana immediately took my mom aside and informed her. Mom immediately went upstairs to check on my sister while I informed dad. He shook his head and let Mom handle it. He thanked Diana for her assistance, and she simply said that it was not a concern.

Then, when I was alone in the kitchen having drinks for Diana and myself, he told me, "Adrienne was seen by us today. I believe she expected you to be there. When you weren't around, she appeared angry."

"How do I see her, Dad? We argued the last time I saw her, and I haven't heard from her again. She should call me because it was her responsibility. I'm sorry, I miss her, but I'm not going to initiate communication. Aside from that, I have Diana's thoughts to remember. It's not reasonable to her; she's aware of what occurred. I'm not trying to do something that would endanger her. She is the first to arrive."

"I see what you mean. I'm just worried about Adrienne. I've known her since she was three years old. But I'm sorry about this schism between you. So I see what you're doing, Jon. Will you worry about it?"

"Dad, I'll pray about it. That's the most I can manage." I returned to the living room with two glasses of iced tea after he nodded. Mom came down a few minutes later and kissed Diana on the face, repeatedly praising her for assisting Cammy, who was asleep.

"Diana, you're a sweetheart. I can't express how grateful I am. Camilla adores you as well."

"I was just happy to be there to assist. Not that Jon couldn't have supported her, but it was simpler for her to support herself with a woman. And I adore her as well. She reminds me of my younger sibling."

We stayed for another half hour until I drove Diana home; it had been a long day, and the heat can be exhausting. Besides, she was heading to my house with her family for a barbeque on Sunday. Not that I wouldn't have preferred to stay the night with them.

I asked her this as we said our goodnights. "Angel, do you suppose we should spend the whole night together tomorrow or

Tuesday? We haven't been out for a night in a long time." I was staring at her almost imploringly.

"Tomorrow evening. My parents would not scold me. They understand how precious you are to me. I need to spend Tuesday alone with my dad, so we can spend the day together on Wednesday as long as we have dinner with my family. Then we'll be quiet for a couple of hours, but I can't stay out that late, Bear. Thursday, I have to get up early. It's like 6 a.m." As we hugged each other, we were very still. "I can't imagine I'll be gone for eight weeks. Over the past six years, I've looked forward to this every season. Every year at this time, I can't wait to get there. And this year, I'm almost looking forward to it. What am I going to do this summer without you?" Diana was weeping once more, and I was crying along with her. Still, I wanted to be there for her and let her leave with a good outlook.

"What's finished is done, honey. I'm sure you will change your mind and spend the whole summer with me. But since I'll be operating throughout the day, you'll have to pursue another career, one that won't be as enjoyable as working at Surprise Lake. And you'll be miserable as a result. That is not what I desire for you, Angel. We'll miss each other terribly, but it's just the season. We'll run into each other again. I guarantee it. If I may, I'll rearrange my vacation days. Whatever it takes for me to see you. I adore you, Diana. With my whole spirit."

She kissed me softly, gently, and sweetly all over my forehead. "Gentle Bear, my great gentle bear. I adore you with all my bones. This is going to be a challenge. If we last the season....."

"If that's the case, we're truly supposed to be. We'll complete this exam with flying colors. You'll see what I mean. And after the summer is done, keep an eye out. I will shut you up in a room and fuck you all day, every day."

Diana chuckled loudly, which warmed my spirit. "You won't have to bind me. I'll be the one that attacks you!" We kissed a couple more times before I had to go. I had to head to the store in the morning to get supplies for my parents' barbeque. Any of our neighbors and relatives would even attend, making it a kind of casual graduation gathering. Mom had bought 40 hot dogs, sandwiches, and Italian sausage, as well as bread, salads, and condiments. Others brought alcohol, wine, soft beverages, paper products, and sweets—a huge group with many people.

When I got home, my parents were already up, wanting to speak to me even after midnight. Mom said after they shared their appreciation for how Diana and I treated Camilla's case once more, "Jon, you must make an effort to make it right with Adrienne. She was devastated because you didn't join us today. I realize she was the one who started the war, and what she expected was irrational. We're proud of you for sticking to your guns and being loyal to Diana. But Adrienne isn't just our friends' daughter; she's been your acquaintance for years. Because of this, Sandy and Marvin will not be arriving tomorrow. Our closest companions. As a result of the two of you."

That hurt me a lot; it wasn't my mom's intention, but it did. "You can't blame that on me, Mom. I'm going to have to worry about Diana. She is now first in my world, aside from my immediate relatives. We're already worried about her leaving for the summer. I don't want to do something that would aggravate our relationship. She'd actually accept if I sorted it out with Adrienne, but she'd be nervous, and Adrienne, after all, should make the first step. It was not my responsibility." I attempted to take a stand.

Dad then spoke up. "I know it sounds a little sexist, but be a grown-up about it, Jon. If you are able, please take the initiative. We brought you up to be a gentleman. Call Adrienne first thing in the morning to want to make it right with her. We'd like them to arrive the next day. They were just three. Will you please?"

I let out a sigh. I was exhausted and wanted to relax. "I need to speak with Diana first. I won't do that until I know she won't get injured. That is everything you would comprehend."

"It's all right," dad said. "I understand; I would do the same if it were my mother. And we see how special she is, as well as how you feel for each other. Simply call as soon as possible." After that, I kissed Mom good night, and we all went to bed.

The next morning, I checked in with Camilla in the kitchen to make sure she was well. She said that she was, and she apologized for wasting my evening. I stood with her as she ate her bagel and advised her not to be stupid, but she didn't do something silly. Diana and I were also relieved to have been there when it occurred.

She sent me a friendly smile and said, "Diana is one of my favorite people, Jon. I'm thrilled you spotted her."

I returned her smile and informed her I was happy I had found her as well. She hugged me, and I softly kissed her back. I then returned to my space with a bottle of juice. I received two tough phone calls.

Diana was the first. I informed her about my chat with my parents after exchanging our I love yous and making some small talk. "Please don't feel pressed here, honey. Tell me if the prospect of meeting Adrienne later leaves you uneasy. My parents are aware that you are the most valuable person in my life. I promised them I wouldn't do something that might damage you."

"I must confess that I wish I didn't have to care about this. And I sound like I'm carrying the whole weight of the world on my back. I almost wish you had just called her and told me later. Yet I'm relieved you didn't. Call her instead. I can't say I fault her for being drawn to you. "She said it as casually as she could. "Maybe the three of us should find a nice spot and chat for a while. If she means something to you, she means something to me."

"Angel, I adore you. Thank you for your patience. My dear, I'll see you at 2 p.m."

"We will be present. And I adore you, Bear."

The next decision was the most difficult. Adrienne detected the third ring. "Hello, Ade. How are you doing?"

"I've been doing well. Ok, for the most part. I've been feeling bad about how I handled you, Jon. I'm so sorry for how I behaved and for not calling you sooner." Then she began to weep, and I let her go for a few moments. Women have been weeping all over me recently.

I finally informed her, "It's all right, Ade. What's gone is gone. I promise we're well. I apologize for not seeing you yesterday. Do you think you and your parents would be able to come to our barbeque this afternoon? We'd both be delighted to see you. Camilla has been missing you as well."

"If Camilla needs to see me, I'm sure we'd be happy to come. Should we have a conversation with Diana? Is she going to be there?"

"She would, indeed. My parents met her parents at graduation, and they both got along well. So her whole family, including her twin brothers, will be there."

"Oh? Are they adorable?"

"Of course, if you want 15-year-olds." We both chuckled, and it feels wonderful to joke again with her. It seemed like an eternity had passed.

I told my friends, who praised me for assisting them. Cammy and I went to the store to get the meats, bread, and salads. She felt much better every day; a little TLC and some assistance from mom had gone a fair way for her.

We had our main grill, plus dad borrowed a pair of barbecue grills from invited neighbors, and at 1:30, he lit the coals to enable them to get white-hot. I took a short shower, and by the time the guests arrived, we were ready to set the table. Diana and her family arrived shortly after 2 p.m. We hugged each other and embraced warmly, though not enthusiastically. We ordered a pair of drinks, and Adrienne and her parents came about ten minutes later. We kissed on the mouth, and she and Diana followed suit, kissing on the cheek and embracing. That gave me optimism for the future for all of us.

When dad, Marvin, and the other men ran the grills, I sat with Ade and Diana, and we all had a heart-to-heart while we ate. There was no animosity, and we did an excellent job in removing the weather. They could never be good buddies, but they might be polite for as long as Diana and I were a couple. Maybe a century.

I got up, offered my father and his friends a break to relax and rest, and worked at the grills with Walt and Will. We kept the food flowing because they had some expertise from their aunt. Then some other men offered us a reprieve, and so on. When I wasn't preparing, I was hanging out with Diana and Ade, and Cammy joined us because we were all among her favorite people. And because we all adored her, we were delighted to have her around.

As the evening progressed, Ade, Diana, and I were buzzed but not intoxicated. It was enjoyable, and they got along well. When the party ended, I walked Adrienne to her parents' vehicle, giving us a few minutes alone to chat.

"Jon, thank you for calling today. I'm sorry for not contacting you first."

"Ade, forget it. It's the past. We're fine."

She embraced and kissed my face, which I returned. It felt good to have my friend back in my life, particularly because she was getting along with Diana. Things could get a lot worse.

Diana and I walked to her house after Diana and her family had left. It was just a 20-minute stroll in either direction, and it was a pleasant evening out. We moved together, holding hands like 15-year-olds falling in love for the first time. We didn't speak about something significant. It was fantastic.

As we arrived at her place, we stood on the steps together, kissing and laughing. "Bear, do you mind if I tell you something?" she asked.

"Angel, you should tell me something. You are aware of this."

"I'm not fond of Adrienne."

That threw me for a loop. "You two got together fantastically tonight. What's the problem?"

"I couldn't place my finger on it." Diana lowered her gaze to where our fingertips were intertwined. "If you asked her, I'm sure she'd answer the same thing if she were truthful. It's a female issue. I'll never forget how she wanted to seduce you not just when you were engaged to me, but even when you promised her you wouldn't cheat on me, and she never apologized; you had to call her. It's certainly not something I'm going to overlook. I'll never lie to you and say we can't see her. She's your mate, and I trust you. Still, I doubt I'll ever be able to do much other than accept her."

"Wow, I must be as deafeningly deafeningly deafeningly deaf I assumed all was well between you two. She didn't say anything as I led her to her vehicle. Are you certain she feels the same way?"

"Almost entirely. Women's intuition is no laughing matter." Diana said it as a prank, but neither her speech nor her eyes were amused. This was serious business.

"Fuck you. How will I be buddies with her? Angel, you mean something to me."

"We can see her together, and you can even visit her this summer when I'm away, but we'll never be friends in our own right. And accept my apologies, Jon. That's just how I felt."

"If that's the case, I'll have to live with it. "You"...a kiss on her nose..." will always"...a little kiss on her lips..."come first." A big kiss was returned with zeal.

We spoke for about ten minutes before I had to go. We decided to spend the night together the next day, Monday, so I wanted to get home, support my parents with whatever was left to clean, and get some sleep. I had a suspicion I wouldn't get anything the next night.

XXXXXXXXXXXXXXXXXXXXXXXXXXXXXXXXXXXXXXXXXX
XXXXXXXXXXXXXXXXXXXXXXXXXXXXXXXXXXXXXXXXXX
XXXXXXXXXXXXXX

Monday, I worked a few hours. I wanted to, so I took off Tuesday and Wednesday to spend as much time as Diana. Sy and Marilyn were sympathetic to my situation; they had met in high school before marrying at 20. They were also grateful that I kept my promise to work for them full-time over the summer, allowing them to plan holidays for their other workers. They informed me many times that I will be missing when I returned to school at the end of August.

When I got home, I took a long hot shower, shaved carefully, and dressed nicely but casually. Tan slacks, a blue and red white button-down top (fashionable 40 years ago), and shoes that aren't sneakers.

Cammy tested me out as I came downstairs and exclaimed, "Hubbahubba!" before rolling on the sofa. I couldn't help but smile; she was having a good time.

"Squirt, I'll know that sometime. When a boy arrives to pick you up for a date, I'll make him so unhappy that he'll run away weeping."

"Whatevs. I'm going to have a lot of options for boyfriends! "She shook her head, batting her eyes. I couldn't stop laughing along with her. When I left, I knew I'd miss her more than my parents.

I held a tiny bag when I kissed mom by the stove and reminded her that I wouldn't be home until the next day. She nodded, acknowledging, not fully agreeing but still not disapproving. It would have been different if Diana had been just a random person I was seeing. They would never have let me spend the night with Diana, no matter how old I was. But they understood our friendship was strong and caring, and they knew the eight weeks would be difficult for me.

I picked Diana up and, after a few kisses around the corner, we went to dinner at a new Japanese restaurant. Japanese food was not as popular back then as it is now. Few people had some clue what sushi was, let alone fried food. As a result, it was going to be an adventure.

We sat in traditional Japanese fashion, with shoes off, legs under the bench, and sitting on cushions. We were given a short tutorial about using chopsticks, which we did pretty well when consuming pickled vegetables. We glanced at the menu, which had nothing recognizable on it, in a daze. We debated it for a long time before deciding that we weren't adventurous enough to eat raw seafood. We decided on Shabu-Shabu, which is a two-person meal. It was described in the explanation how it is cooked at the table.

We thought that meant a waiter would prepare it for us, but that wasn't the case. They put an electric pot between us to heat water, and then two trays, one of the raw meats and the other of raw vegetables, both thinly cut, arrived, along with bowls of sauces for dipping. Diana and I exchanged wary glances; we were supposed to prepare our meals. We had little idea how to boil beef, how long it might take, or what the sauces were, and the workers spoke no English. To tell it was a fun encounter will be an understatement. It was a nightmare for us, with chewy beef, overcooked vegetables, and foreign sauces.

We finished our meal, I paid the bill, and we were on our way out. We were screaming like insane people as soon as we walked out of the house. "Oh my God, that was incredible!" I tried and failed to maintain a regular expression.

Diana wasn't any different. "Never, ever again! I can never consume Shitsu-Shitsu again!" and we all burst out laughing. "Do you want something to eat, Bear?"

"I'm starving! Let's go to Amore for a delicious pizza!" So we went to Amore and finished our Japanese trip with some nice pizza (nowadays, I can't go two weeks without having sushi or hibachi chicken and shrimp). But it is no longer the case.) We noticed a couple of friends from school having slices and invited them to sit with us as we spoke about our summer plans.

"It was the most luxurious pizza dinner I've ever had," I said in the taxi.

"Yes, thirty dollars for four slices of pizza. What a steal."

"I'm not bothered. Not until I have the opportunity to be with you, my Angel. Every second is priceless."

Diana stared at me with those light blue eyes that make my heart skip a beat. "You're such a nice guy. Gentle Bear, please." Diana, my petite sweet baby, drew me close and kissed me sweetly and lovingly. It was fortunate that we were affectionate individuals; it turned out very well for both of us. "Sweetheart, please take me somewhere where we can be alone. I want to get you out of your clothing and into my body. So many occasions as you possibly can. We may not even be able to sleep tonight."

"Angel, that is enticing. Do you like going anywhere a bit more cheesy than the Holiday Inn?"

"Right now, you should carry me to a closet, and I wouldn't say something." I shivered in her embrace as she kissed my neck with her warm, red lips. I rode as far as I could, though remaining secure to a cheap motel near LaGuardia Airport, which was just ten minutes away. When I pulled up next to Diana's office, she laughed and said, "When you said cheesy, I didn't realize you meant Limburger." We didn't mind as long as it was safe. However, this was a low-cost establishment. I was attempting to survive on a tight budget.

The space was tidy, but it was extremely cheesy. Fake wood paneling on the doors, a tiny dresser and night tables, and a bathroom smaller than a walk-in wardrobe, complete with toilet, bathtub, and sink. It would have been unlikely if we had been on the road. But we were staying for the weekend.

Diana excused herself to the toilet as I sat on the bed waiting. It caused some small squeaking noises when I sat down, so I jumped slightly, and the springs objected. I felt I could have splurged a little more for a nicer bed. Diana emerged from the restroom wearing a slinky off-white negligee and sheer pantyhose. For the time being, I've forgotten about the mattress. "Diana, my Angel....you never fail to steal my breath away."

"I'm hoping for a split second. I'd hate to murder you too quickly after discovering you." She grinned as she approached me and kissed me softly. "Do you need to go to the restroom before I devour you?"

"Yes, just a few moments. Don't leave the house without me!" I kissed her back and walked away with my little purse. I had a little treat in store for her. I went to the restroom for a moment before changing into something fun for her, a pair of black satin boxer shorts. I'd been holding them for the perfect night, and this seemed to be it.

When I returned, Diana was lying back on the bed, saying to herself, "You sure went all out on this bed, didn't you, my Gent...?" She came to a halt when she noticed me in my boxers. "That's incredible. Now it's my turn to be out of breath. Bear, that is sexy. Maybe you don't want to be too gentle this time around?" Diana raised her eyebrows.

"I can be your gentle bear or your ferocious bear. You have the choice of being my Angel or my little Devil. But for the time being, what I want is you, my heart, my true love." I crawled into the noisy bed into Diana's big open arms, and we kissed each other long, lovingly, intensely. Our bodies brushed up against each other, heightening our sexual appetite and hunger. We were kissing and nibbling, also lightly chewing, as our heat increased. We would have melted together if the air conditioner in the room had not fitted.

"Bear, take off my nightgown. Please suck my breasts, "Diana begged. We were aching for each other, but we needed it to continue as long as possible to get as much satisfaction from each other as possible. I pulled the flimsy top piece above her head and sucked instinctively at her left breast.

"Don't wait, boy," she said repeatedly, and I had no intention of stopping.

"You don't either," I said into her ear.

"I'm not going to do that; I'm not going to do that." Her eyes were tightly closed but opened wide, her mouth met mine, and Diana climbed onto my fingertips in her pantyhose. I find myself ejaculating big, creamy strings of semen in my shorts and all over her fragile hand because the fragrance was amazing. It wasn't quite as satisfying as raping each other. However, it came close. We were exhausted for the time being, though not quite enough for the evening.

We were huddled together, sweaty all over, and overjoyed. We kissed each other all over our faces and upper bodies. "That was amazing, my Angel. It's really interesting. My darling, I adore you."

"Oh, my great sexy Bear, I approve. That is all we would repeat. Once more, "With a sweet and sexy joke, she added. And she stumbled sideways into the bunk, which creaked harshly. "I understand you're trying to save space, sweetheart, but I have a feeling this bed won't like what we're about to do to it later."

I shared a joke with her and said, "So be it if we crack it. They do not have a credit card issued by us. Let's give it our everything!" Diana chuckled from my lips and beard from the ticklish sensations when I assaulted her, kissing all over her chest and stomach.

"Stop, you insane beast! You're going to get me to pee!" She couldn't help laughing and swatted my ass in amusement.

I stood up and exclaimed, "It is not what I like in our room! This isn't the kind of place that would give housekeeping in the middle of the night! Go ahead and piss in the bathroom!" She stood up, and I gently spanked her when she passed by, sending me a funny/dirty look as we moved.

Diana gently climbed into bed with me when she returned. We were both terrified that any rash romantic moves would shatter the room. We snuggled together for the time being, both in our very sweaty clothing, which was becoming awkward, so we stripped nude, both for warmth and practicality. We had some pillow chat, mainly Diana telling me about the people she was excited to see and hear campers, some of whom were children when she began and will now be Counselors in Training. Her happiness was so palpable that I realized it was the best decision to ask her to stick to her plans. Missing her would be difficult, but we'd be together all year after the summer. Diana couldn't reclaim the summer if she missed it.

I suppose I let her do most of the talking. She finally said something after a while "What about the bear? Are you on board with me?" Her hand caressed my chest.

"My Angel, of course. I was paying close attention to every expression. I was just hoping that going to camp would be a good idea for you. I wish you could see how your eyes light up as you discuss it. That was everything I couldn't take away from you. If I did, I'd sound like a jerk. I'll miss you, so this is just what you should be doing. I know it in my bones."

Diana sighed, clutching me tightly. "Why do you have to be so soft, Jon? This would be so much better if you weren't such a jerk."

"Yeah, but aren't you happy I'm not a bit of a prick?" I said it with a devilish grin, pulling my mustache like an old-school movie villain.

"You have no idea. You're perfect for me. As if it were a blade in a sheath. "In truth," she said as she moved to straddle my torso, "why don't we use the sword?" I'm not through with you for the night." Diana leaned in to kiss my mouth, then my jaw, and finally my throat.

"That's a fantastic concept, in my opinion. But first," I drew her up to my face, "let me try something tasty other than your kisses." I nibbled gently on her right calf.

"Oh, you naughty lad. I can't refuse this bid, "Diana said as she brushed back her long, straight hair. I kissed her calves, tasting the residue of her juices that had pooled there, then she bent over and hugged the headboard as I kissed her mound with the soft hairs there. Diana mocked protested, "Bear, you're teasing me."

"Don't you like it when I tease you?"

"Don't give up, boy! Don't even think about stopping!" Diana arrived a few minutes later, a surge of desire rushing through her body and mind, and she thrust down hard, once, twice, and on the third occasion, the bed gave way and fell to the floor. We all burst out laughing because we were already only eight inches lower to the surface. "Fuck, I KNEW that bed wasn't going to last the night!" We couldn't get enough of each other's laughter. It was way too amusing.

"We'll have plenty to say our mates on how we're such beasts that we broke a bed while having sex!" Diana landed on top of me, already laughing loudly. If any guy had sat there alone and jerked off, the bed would have most likely broken.

We cuddled through our giggles and kissed tiny kisses, but our giggles never stopped. This was everything we'd consider for the rest of our lives. My eyes widened as this fresh, incredible pleasure coursed through my body. Diana licked her thumb seductively when things got a little dry, also with my cum dripping, then began rubbing again, shifting ways.

I reached for her, wanting to hug and kiss her, but Diana clearly said, "Uh, uh, uh, uh, uh, Get fun. For the time being." I built up a head of steam, almost to a shaking climax, and then she stopped, allowing me to shake with rage and excitement. She sat there innocently laughing at me, then she began again, this time using her skin cream for lubrication, and again, and again, and again, and again, and again, and again, and again, and again, and again, and again, and again, and again, and again, and again, and

Her hands were on my upper arms, my upper body was about a foot away from hers, and I maintained that position as we quietly looked into each other's eyes. I'm not sure how long I remained like that for, maybe a minute or five. I had no idea; we were just swept up in the ecstasy of our passion and desire. I eventually rolled to the left to avoid collapsing on top of her and injuring her. I will never do something that would deliberately or unintentionally damage Diana. Never, ever.

We huddled together, our sweat making the room seem cold. We remained quiet, speaking only through our eyes and kisses.

Diana muttered, "You adore kissing me, don't you? Don't worry; I'm not grumbling."

"I'm making amends for the many years we've known each other but never kissed. We're only nine years late, in my opinion."

"Do you want to make up for those nine mistakes tonight? And it is what appeals to me." My Angel embraced me many times, and we laughed together. The sex, the loving, and the sheer enjoyable and amusing circumstances were all leading to this being one of the greatest nights in each of our lives. We were making the most of the night, which may have been our last together for a long time.

We sat in the collapsing bunk, smiling at each other and kissing intermittently. And if it was late, we weren't sleepy. We thought we wanted and take a shower to get rid of the stickiness before heading to bed, so we crammed into the cramped shower stall and got washed despite the low water pressure and cold water. We dried off (barely) with the threadbare towels, and Diana said, "No offense, Bear, but if you carry me back to this dump again, you'll be playing with yourself for a long time." It would have been quite amusing if we hadn't known I'd be playing with myself a lot over the summer. "I'm so sorry, Jon. I didn't give any thought about what I was doing."

"It's all right, Angel. I suppose I earned it. This place is so bad it's amusing, like something out of an Ed Wood film. I could have invested the additional $20 in a better hotel. I reasoned that what we wanted were a bed and a toilet. That's what I get for pretending to be a cheapskate."

Diana walked up behind me, put her towel around her waist, and embraced me from behind. As she laid her head on my shoulder, I squeezed her hands. It was both romantic and moving. Her affection washed through me, and I sobbed quietly about how I had fucked up the night. She forced me to turn back to face her. "Gentle Bear, this has been one of the happiest nights of my life. We've had a couple of laughs to go along with some pretty amazing sex. And if you're really up for it, we're not finished yet. So there will be no more tears. My great little Gentle Bear, I love you more than anything in the universe."

"Angel, I adore you as well. You are my whole universe. My whole being. I'm going to miss you terribly. Let me carry you back to your bed....whatever that is." Diana giggled as I scooped her up in my arms like a groom taking his wife over a threshold. As we arrived at the shabby room, I let her down gently before taking off our towels and letting the joy wash through us once more.

"Bear, take a seat. Allow me to do a wonderful service for you."

"You've always done too much for me."

"Not this evening, not yet. Just relax and have fun. Please allow me." Diana continued to kiss my chest, paying special attention to my nipples, which were not as responsive as hers, but it was always really exciting for me. She worked her way down my torso steadily, teasing me in the vulnerable region between my belly button and pubic hair, causing me to shiver and shake. And sigh uncontrollably.

"You're incredible, my naughty little Devil. You make me sound fantastic. Almost often "slowly engulfing me before she worked the head into her throat "Unnngggghhhh" was the only sound I could create, particularly when she swallowed, an amazing sensation that elevated me to a new level of pleasure. My whole body was trembling, like a quivering ball of jello. That was how good my Angel was at serving me. She kept pushing me back so she could breathe, then back into her throat until I was hers to do whatever she wanted with. I might have been done by now if it hadn't been for my two recent orgasms. I had her off of me until I offered her a huge creamy load and asked, "What can I do to help you, Angel? I'm willing to do whatever you ask. All go."

Diana turned around and kissed me before laying prone on her front on the bunk. "Use your skills to get me steaming hot before you fuck me like this, my sexy Bear. My skin is tingling just thinking about it!"

Whatever she fancied. I kissed her from the back of her neck to the top of her back, then down her spine. My right hand's fingertips ran softly along her lower lips as they were between her spread thighs. She squirmed about, a wide grin on her pretty lips, her eyes closed in a relaxed pose. "Bear, you're doing fantastic. Wonderfully done."

"Thank you very much, Angel. It's both my fun and yours. Maybe even more, "I said this while licking her cheeks.

"That's great. I want you to be a part of me for the rest of my life, "With a gentle chuckle, she said. "I never want to lose you. I'll even take you to camp with me like this. "She chuckled even harder, wiggling her sexy little butt.

"They could shoot you," I grumbled as I kissed her shoulder.

"Oh right, we'll just be together all the time!"

I gave her a soft spanking, and she let me move, and my Angel moaned as I grasped her hips and gently pumped her, feeling the fire rise in both of us. When my groin slapped on her pretty round bottom, I eventually picked up my pace, creating slapping noises with my groin. My thighs pushed hers wider again, and I fucked her deeper and harder, both of us grunting and moaning before she arrived. "Jon, my hottie! Don't cum yet, please! Pull out as soon as possible!"

Diana let me go, and we immediately settled in close to hug and kiss each other. I ran my fingertips through her hair and whispered to her, "My Angel, I adore you. I'm fairly confident I'll love you for the rest of my life."

Diana smiled sweetly as she glanced up at me. "I believe I will always love you, Gentle Bear. Forever and ever. And you're such a wonderful lover. Always my Gentle Bear, except you seem to recognize when I want anything more. I never have to remind you of something. My hottie." She kissed my sternum. "I can't picture any other guy being as in tune with me as he is."

We moved in, took turns using the wardrobe, er, toilet, and returned to the ground bed on the low, making us laugh again. We'd be joking over it if we lived to be 90 and were all together. It had been one of the most enjoyable nights any of us had ever experienced, but it was time to relax. We were looking forward to waking up together.

XXXXXXXXXXXXXXXXXXXXXXXXXXXXXXXXXXXXXXXXXXX
XXXXXXXXXXXXXXXXXXXXXXXXXXXXXXXXXXXXXXXXXXX
XXXXXXXXXXXXXXXXXXXXXX

We awoke around 9 a.m., and after another trip to the toilet, we lay in bed and thought about nothing significant. It didn't take long for our libidos to take over, and we made love slowly and sweetly. It was the perfect way to round off our overnight together.

We scrambled to get ready in the aftermath, not remembering we had to check out by 11 a.m. or I'd be stuck for a second day. Not in that shambles of a bed. We went out for breakfast on Diana after moving out. I ordered a large stack of pancakes, although she ordered a short stack. When we were done, we had a serious conversation about coffee and tea.

"Will I be able to see you tonight? I remember we decided you'd be with your family tomorrow. We should keep things easy by going to the movies."

"That is perfectly acceptable to me. A movie looks fantastic. Maybe the Alien film that everybody is talking about? I like a strong, scary film."

"Will miracles never end? Sure, if you can have it, I'll take it."
We sipped our beverages in silence for a moment. "Angel, I'm
going to miss you. I can't picture how it would be without you.
We can't speak on the phone at night. How much will you
contact me?"

"Maybe twice a week. Mondays and Thursdays, I will call my
parents and you. Each session will last five minutes. Only
enough time to continue and plan our vacation days." She took a
sip of her coffee. "That's going to irritate me. It's much worse for
you; I'm surrounded by campers and mates every day and night.
I'm feeling crappy about it. I sincerely hope you will be able to
attend next week."

"The same thing happened to me. It's the one thing that'll keep
me sane. If you want to leave me that pair of pants?" With a sad
smile, I said.

"With much joy. That way, I know you'll remember me if
you....you know."

"I wish I didn't have to....you see," I joked.

"At the very least, you have a lot of privacy to....you see."
Masturbation was becoming an amusing euphemism for us. "In
my bunk, I have a different space from the ladies so that you can

hear anything. When I....you see, I have to cram a pillow in my mouth." We were all laughing at this stage. "Seriously, none of us should have to. I wish we could spend every night and every day together whenever we like. Or to simply cuddle whenever we like. Even just to learn about it." Diana was weeping, only tears streaming down her beautiful face, but it bothered me to see her in pain. I took her hand in mine, and our fingers were intertwined.

"Take a look at me, Angel." Her gaze was drawn to mine as she wiped her eyes with the other hand's napkin. "We're going to do it. You're leaving for the summer, so it's not like I won't be able to get there in a reasonable period. We may not see each other every week, but we can. I'll go there next week if I can. When you come home, we'll have more than a week before school starts, and we'll spend as much time as we can together. We'll figure it out." I was just doing that for Diana's sake, so I was starving on the inside. I despised it almost as much as she did. Still, we had no choice but to accept it.

We wrapped our arms around each other's waists as we walked to my vehicle. Diana turned quickly and embraced me tightly as we approached the vehicle. "Thank you so much, Gentle Bear. I realize you're as mad as I am, and you're just trying to make it better for me. It means a lot to me. You're one out of a million."

I kept her in the parking lot, unconcerned with whether or not people stared. Nothing was more important to me than Diana. My mates, or similarly so. It would have been a difficult decision that I was fortunate not to have to make. "How do I deceive you?"

"There is no way. I know your heart as well as you know mine. Yet, I admire your efforts. Jon, I adore you. Bear, my huge, sweet bear."

"My Angel, I adore you as well. To the moon and back."

XXXXXXXXXXXXXXXXXXXXXXXXXXXXXXXXXXXXXXXXXXXX
XXXXXXXXXXXXXXXXXXXXXXXXXXXXXXXXXXXXXXXXXXXX
XXXXXXXXXXXXXX

I drove Diana home and, after doing some housework and changing the oil in my vehicle, I showered, changed into jeans and a t-shirt, and finally had dinner with my dad. They realized that I hadn't been around much this week. I took Diana to see Alien (Cammy wanted to go, but my parents said no way, no R-rated movies for her yet) and, apart from being terrified, we had a nice time just seeing a video. After that, we went out for ice cream (it was a really hot night) and called it a night. We were also exhausted. We didn't see each other on Tuesday. I had to sleep, and she had some last-minute shopping to do, so she spent the night with her parents and brothers playing a board game and watching a video, something they used to do a lot before I came into her life. I went to hang out with Mike and a couple of people, which I hadn't done in a while but planned to do a lot this summer.

We spent the whole day together on Wednesday. Her brothers were away at a teen day-only sports camp for the summer (Cammy was at the same camp, in their Tweens program), so Diana and I took advantage, having very uninhibited sex in her room. Then she spent the afternoon preparing her suitcases from a list, and I assisted as well as I could. We didn't say anything because it weighed heavily on us. We had dinner with her dad, and he came by my house to say farewell to my family for the season. Cammy was in a bad mood. She and Diana were like mothers, and Diana was depressed as well. They promised to write to each other, and we left to spend some time alone. I wanted to send her home by midnight so she could relax.

We parked in "our place" and had our first kiss in my car. We moved slowly, tenderly, and lovingly. We kissed at least a hundred times. Her breasts rubbed against my sweaty stomach, and her knees rubbed against my thighs and cheeks. We made the most of it, and we didn't know how long it would be until we had another shot. When we did get together, it wasn't spectacular. Instead, it was lovely. It looked fine, and it felt much stronger internally. And so, when it was after 11 p.m. when we realized we had to start getting ready to go home, we all fell apart. We cried in each other's arms for the pain we were both feeling inside.

At 11:30, I said, "We have to get moving, Angel. You're going to need some rest overnight."

"Do you believe I'll be able to sleep tonight, Bear? Perhaps a couple of hours. I'm terrified that I'll miss you. I'm terrified."

"That's not going to happen, honey. I'm not touching or even looking at another girl. I'm afraid not. I'm not going to."
Diana kissed me again, this time strongly. "I understand, Bear. Yet I'm also terrified."
"I understand. I'm terrified as well. I'm afraid of missing you. You'll encounter all those hot men, some of whom have already been in college for a year or two. They may be appealing. I'm aware of it."

"No way, no how. I don't want someone else but you, Jon. Not today, and never before." We disentangled ourselves and dressed to go home, although reluctantly. Diana had assumed she wouldn't see me for at least a week, so I would impress her by showing up at the parking lot where the staff assembled to board buses to the camp. One more short farewell.

When we arrived at her home, we stood by her entrance, saying our goodbyes. We couldn't articulate anything other than "I love you."

I didn't want to surprise her. "How about I pick you up, save your father's time, and drive you to the meeting place? We should utter our last goodbyes."

"Are you serious? Look how difficult it was tonight. If you want to look over it again in the morning?"

"I do, indeed. I'd take any moment I might spend with you. I'll pick you up at 7 a.m., and we will have breakfast on the way."

"Okay. Carry it out. Please pick me up. Bear, you know how much I adore you. Much than I imagined was feasible."

"The same thing happened to me. I never imagined I might love anyone as much as I love you. Return to. Please arrive at 7 a.m. Attempt to get some rest." I went home, hurting on the inside, after one more kiss. One last day to see her. It proved to be my savior.

XXXXXXXXXXXXXXXXXXXXXXXXXXXXXXXXXXXXXXXXXXX
XXXXXXXXXXXXXXXXXXXXXXXXXXXXXXXXXXXXXXXXXXX
XXXXXXXXXXXXXXXXXXXXX

I arrived at her house at 7 a.m., politely knocked, and Diana let me in with a kiss, looking like she got almost the same amount of sleep as I had about 2 hours. She embraced and kissed her parents and brothers as I carried most of her belongings to my vehicle. The important ones. Her parents waived farewell, saying they'd see her on Parents Day, the first weekend of August. We drove to a nearby deli where they delivered what could only be found in a New York deli: two bacon, egg, and cheese sandwiches on hard rolls, often known as Kaiser rolls—served with chocolate. We weren't hungry, so we had to feed. So we ate a little something.

When we arrived at the parking lot, I parked farthest away from the meeting spot, and we said a more subdued farewell. It was still excruciatingly painful. After nearly halving the time, I drove to where the buses were waiting for the workers and assisted in getting her luggage out. Someone helped them into the bus, and our last farewell was emotional, but not in front of her peers. "Please call me on Sunday and let me know when I will see you. I adore you to the moon and beyond."

"I'll call you. I want to do so. Jon, I adore you. My whole core." The horn sounded, and she knew she had to get on the bus. She got on, walked over to a window, and said, "I love you, Bear!!!"

"I adore you as well!!! Get a safe journey!!!" "Diana's got a bookyyyyyyyyyyyyyyyyyyyyyyyyyyyyyyyyyyyyyyyyyyyyyyyyyyyyyyyyy yyyyyyy I laughed at her plight. They can just bust your balls if they are in love with you. She was out with her parents. It was going to be a nice, hot summer for me. Quite LONG.

I stayed in my seat, watching the buses exit the parking lot and hearing Diana's friends teasing her about our passionate farewell in front of everyone. Later, I discovered that her lifetime friends were a mix of thrilled and a little jealous because she was clearly in love. It was all in good fun, and Diana told them our tale on the way up (just the high points, leaving out very personal things...I think).

I tried to exit the parking lot after the buses had gone, but I couldn't get out right away. I had to pull over because I was weeping and missing her. It took me a few moments to regain my equilibrium. I didn't mind if someone saw me. The effect of not having Diana for the majority of the summer was devastating, and it struck me like a ton of bricks.

I had a half-hour until college, so I went early. Cammy was the only one there, and I held her tightly. She understood what was killing me because she was my loving and adoring little sister, and she only kissed me as I had done with her countless times over the years.

"I'm sorry, Jon; I know you'll miss Diana; I'll miss her as well, but it won't be the same. But you'll see her again, and then you'll be back together. Meanwhile, you have me to adore. Jon, I've lost my me and your, period." She backed up far enough to throw me a wide grin. Damn, she was maturing into a woman rather than a boy, in her heart rather than in her physical growth. To let you know, we're all very good friends and siblings after more than 40 years. That's how it's always been.

"Thank you, Cammy. That makes me feel a lot easier. We'll do something at least once a week, or go to a movie or get pizza. It's a Mets puzzle. We will go when the Dodgers come to town next week." She cracked a big smile at that. And I did feel a bit happier after that. It's not anything, but it's anything.

So the summer began. I started working full-time on Thursday, and Sy and Marilyn were as accommodating as they could be in offering me a day off each week to travel upstate to see Diana. Diana sent me the days every Monday night, except the first time I talked to her on Sunday night, the day before camp began.

The first week, she didn't have a day off, which was a total bummer for both of us because we couldn't see each other until the next Tuesday. It was difficult. The positive news was that they allowed her to take two days off two weeks later to see the Grateful Dead concert on Monday and spend the night and all day Tuesday together.

I was up really early on the first day, Tuesday the 10th. The night before, I couldn't relax. I left at 7 a.m., and after facing traffic for most of the route, I arrived at the office before 9 a.m., a little early, and went into the office to wait for her.

I introduced myself to the individual behind the desk and explained why I was there. He shook my hand and said Diana might take me around if I liked. Maybe someday, I thought, and then Diana came in, and it was everything I could do not to sweep her up in my arms and embrace her passionately in front of the four or five people there.

"Hi honey," I managed to say with a shaky voice before embracing her with less than a tenth of my passion for her.

"Hello, sweetheart," she said with a tender yet caring embrace. We embraced hard, not knowing who saw or what gossip could be shared after we left. It felt amazing to have her back in my arms after nearly two weeks away.

90

"Ahem," Lenny (the man behind the desk) cleared his throat, a grin on his face. I'm sure he'd seen it before; I discovered he was about 40 years old and had been with the camp for nearly 20 years, working his way up to the assistant director.

"We're behaving, Lenny," Diana said, a wide grin on her face. "Did you have breakfast?"

"No, it does not. I needed to arrive as soon as possible."

"Do you mind if I take Jon over to the dining hall and see what they still have left from breakfast?" Diana asked Lenny.

"Diana, you can proceed. At the very least, there's cold cereal, if not something warmer. It was a pleasure to meet you, Jon. Diana, please return here by 9 p.m. tonight."

"I want to do so. Thank you, Lenny." She took my hand and guided me outside behind the office, where we kissed properly in private. We exchanged a big embrace, followed by another and another. "Bear, I can't believe you're here. I've been missing you terribly."

"I understand. I've been keeping track of the days. I'm not sure how long I slept last night, but it wasn't much. My Guardian Angel. I adore you to the moon and beyond!"

"I adore you, my dear Bear." Another pair of kisses. "Let's go find you something to eat. You'll use all of your courage today!" We made a wonderful sound as we chuckled together. We encountered more than a dozen staff members walking with children on the way to the dining hall, and Diana introduced me to everyone, but I couldn't recall their names. It was a lovely atmosphere, with gentle hills and greenery anywhere you looked. The structures were all made of white wood with dark green trim. There was a beach and a large lake (Surprise Lake, right?) with rowboats and canoes. There are a few baseball diamonds, squash courts, and basketball courts, as well as a tiny amphitheater by the lake for concerts and plays. It was picture-perfect. I could see why Diana looked forward to working there every season.

When Diana and I arrived at the dining hall, she asked one of the cooks if he could make me some eggs and turkey bacon. Sure, he replied, just sit down, and he'd carry it out in a couple of minutes. We sat at a table and spoke as waiters set up for lunch in a couple of hours. We couldn't quit laughing and smiling; it was fun just to be together. The cook gave me a tray of scrambled eggs and turkey bacon (most Jewish camps hold

Kosher), as well as four pieces of wheat toast. I was hungry enough to finish the last morsel.

When we were there, her party arrived with her two assistant counselors; all of the girls, like Cammy, were around 12 years old, and they all made a huge deal about me, telling me how wonderful Diana was and how thankful they were to me for allowing her to be their mentor for the summer. She was blushing with humiliation, so I thought it was cute that they wanted to tell me how much fun they were having. And there was nothing phony about it; the girls were fond of her, and I realized I was doing the right thing by inviting her to work there for the summer. She and I might be together for years, if not decades. But Diana was making a change in the lives of those children, and I was so proud of her.

"Thank you very much for helping me feel so at home here. I'm happy Diana is making your summer so enjoyable. It makes me miss her a little bit less. But it would help if you realized that I always miss her. I think she's pretty cool, too." When I ended my meal, we held hands around the bar.

"All right, ladies," Diana said to her campers and assistants. "I'm happy you came by, but it's time for me to go play basketball. I'll see you later tonight. I'll be there before bed search, and you can inform me how much fun you had without me." The girls all came down to the basketball court and offered her a group embrace. Diana took my plate and tray, and we returned to the parking lot and the driveway. She slipped next to me, took my right arm as I drove, and led me to a Cold Spring motel.

"The girls adore you," I said as I followed her instructions. "They have excellent taste." I smiled at her, turning my head for a split second so she could see it.

"They'd have a wonderful time regardless of who their psychologist was. I'm also the one they've allocated to this summer."

"Do you think that, Diana? Is there any psychologist that will be as successful and popular with your girls?" I drove into the motel parking lot and stopped, but we remained inside and talked.

"I'm not sure. I believe so." Diana's vulnerability was showing in her self-assurance.

"Let me tell you a story, honey. I noticed their expressions. I also remember you didn't invite them to visit me. It wasn't even the thought of the secretary. Those girls were eager to participate. They needed me to realize how much they appreciate you and make such a difference in their lives. Don't even presume for a second that you're like every other psychologist to them. They are devoted to you. And I'm sure you do as well. Do not even attempt to refute it. And I can see why you enjoy your work so much. It's a lovely spot to spend the season."

"I adore them. It's enjoyable to play games and sing songs. But I enjoy it when I can assist one of them with a problem, even Cindy or Tamara, my assistants. Nothing compares to that sensation. Thank you, Jon. Maybe I'm a little smarter in books, but you see things about people I don't. And you have a keen eye for me. Better than I perceive myself to be." Diana kissed me and held me for a minute.

I went to get a room, but she stopped me and took care of it. "I insist, sweetheart. Please let me. I'm just so glad you're here!" and she got out before I could object.

Diana came out three minutes later and led me to room 115, which was on the 'down' side and much quieter. Or it will be before we arrived. We used the key to unlock the entrance, and before it closed behind us, our lips were sealed, and our clothes were falling off.

"My Angel, I've been looking forward to this for days. I can't get you out of my head. "Between kisses; I told Diana.

"Every night, when I'm alone in my room, I think of you. I'm doing whatever I can to take my hands off myself while dreaming about you." Our kisses were arriving in quick succession, and our passion was certainly higher than it had been since the beginning of our partnership. We were nude and playing about on the bed in two minutes. We were too hot to go slowly.

We both gasped as the old, yet long-forgotten sensation overtook us. Diana wrapped her arms around my neck and raised her hips to match my thrust. Her legs were wrapped around my a$$, drawing me in and still leaving me there. Her legs and body became tighter than they had been only a few weeks before due to the everyday tasks. Not that I didn't already believe she was amazing. But this was something unique.

We moved in unison, our rhythm so natural and easy to find. I must admit that it was a very fast rhythm. We weren't looking for a leisurely pace here, at least not this time. My hips smacked into hers, echoing around the room. I kissed her tight, time after time, our lips so close to each other that I was surprised they weren't bleeding. Then we hit top speed, and we were seconds away from climaxing together.

"Bear, try much harder if you can! Baby, I want to cum with you!"

"Almost there, Angel! We're almost there..."

"My sexy friend, Cum! Please put me in now!" She was moaning and coughing, and it was so surreal to see and sound that I had to join her, which I did. My sperm's heat set her off once more. Diana drew me close to her and embraced me as though it were our last kiss ever. Her eyes were welling up with tears, and I was becoming a bit teary too. Our orgasms were fantastic, just what we wanted. I rolled onto my back, pulling Diana with me, and she sat on top of me. If you can believe it, our kisses were much more wonderful than our sex.

We were huddling together as though we wanted to stay safe, but our closeness was due to the need to bond emotionally. Diana's head was on my lap, her fingertips teasing the hairs on my chest, and I could sense her breath rushing through my hairs. I was tickling her spine up and down to just above her smooth cheeks, and I could detect the jasmine and fruit perfume in her fur. We both missed the intimacy more than anything else. "My Angel, I adore you. I can't even try to tell you."

"You are free to experiment as much as you can. My great Gentle Bear, I love it when you say something like that to me. I'm delighted you've arrived. I'm busy all day and evening, but I do have time to think about you. And, later that night... I miss you very much. And I adore you so much that it hurts."

"I know, but to be honest, after meeting your campers today, I'm happy you're doing this. Those ladies adore you. You're having a wonderful time with them. We'll have lots of time together until the summer is through. We'll have the whole year ahead of us, and probably even more. But right now, you're doing something crucial. Those girls need your assistance."

She grinned at me as she sat back on one elbow. "Bear, I'm so fortunate. You're fortunate to be both selfless and compassionate. Knowing how much you love me makes things simpler for me to stay gone. I wish you were here with me all the time, particularly at night, "Diana commented with a twinkle in her eye. "I'd love to make love to you here under the stars. Your passion, on the other hand, makes this split bearable. And the kids are fantastic. I'm having a great time, though I'm exhausted at night. So, what's going on with your parents and Camilla?"

That sparked a discussion regarding our family, and I realized I had a letter from Camilla for Diana. She read it then and then. She refused to tell me what was in it, claiming it was a private matter between her and my sister. I could see it had an impact on her. "Tell Camilla that I'll write her this week; I'll do it after my kids have gone to bed."

We lay in bed talking, catching up on two weeks of mostly minor events, telling her how I was keeping busy, the friends I hung out with, taking Camilla to dinners and a couple of ball games, and quiet nights at home. She told me about her camp experiences and how her closest friends reacted to her serious boyfriend (they were thrilled for her). They probed her with questions, mainly regarding sex, to which she refused to respond. Girls can be very similar to boys in this way. And neither of us revealed anything to our friends. We were mature enough to keep it to ourselves.

Diana said, "You are welcome to join us on Family Day, which is on Sunday, September 29th. Even my family isn't invited; neither is the staff's family, but I asked Lenny if you should come. We'll bring you a t-shirt and invite you to join us for the day's events. Please react positively."

Her eyes begged me to listen to them. I snatched her palms in mine. "Diana, my Guardian Angel. Attempt to hold me at bay. I'll get a bit more fun with you, and I'll be able to see your mates and spend the day outside in the heat. That's a godsend for somebody who's been trapped in a hot printing plant all day." I embraced her, and we kissed carelessly.

"Thank you so much, Bear. Bear, my huge sexy bear." She smeared kisses all over my chest, which I thoroughly enjoyed. I had the most fun being with Diana. She was a fantasy come true for me.

99

We soon began kissing daily, and one thing led to another. I kissed my way down her body until our arousal had returned. Diana shivered when I touched her most vulnerable regions, which I was well aware of by that point. Her breasts and stomach, for example, were noticeable, but she also enjoyed being kissed at the inner curve of her thigh, just above where her butt started. As I kissed her there, her whole body spasmed, and noisy and sensual noises emanated from deep inside her breast. It was ticklish for her to touch her there, but kissing her there sent her into a whirlwind.

"My lovely Angel. I adore you, darling, and I wish to offer you a great deal of joy. Still only gradually. I'm going to tease you mercilessly!" I said with a wicked grin and sound.

"You're so naughty," she exclaimed, panting. "This is how you tease your adoring girlfriend. If you don't let me cum enough, I may forget you the rest of the day. That is the cock. I'll adore the lot of you." Diana had a dreamy yet needy quality to her voice, trapped between need and peak. I resolved to start offering her everything she so badly desired because I wished the same thing for her. Diana screamed as her body rocked with orgasm as I swirled the tip of my tongue across her clit. The sudden touch had a significant impact on her.

"That was awesome, Jon! More, please? What about me? You're a sweetheart, don't you?"

"Who is who?" I laughed, understanding just what she was joking about.

"The babe who has taught you some new tricks over the last two weeks! Seriously, you sexy Bear, if I didn't know better... I can't believe what you did to me." She kissed me all over my forehead, and I kissed her right back, kiss for kiss. "Every day, Jon, I fall more in love with you. You do the most incredible stuff to me."

"You are an inspiration to me, honey. I only have this incredible need to make you comfortable." She wrapped her arms around me and held me closely.

"Mission achieved!" she exclaimed, smothering me with kisses. "It's now my turn to look after you. I'm just sad I can't reciprocate what you've done for me. It is the fault of biology."
"Whatever you try to do to me, my Angel, I'll gladly agree." I've never had a complaint about how much you support me."
Diana rolled me onto my back and slipped between my thighs. "All right, I'll strive to do something unique for you. Take that as

a matter of honor." Her tongue randomly slithered out and lathered up my glans to a gleaming, glowing crimson. She was off to a fantastic start.

I moaned, often with my eyes firmly shut, often completely open, while I watched my Angel-Devil use her lips and tongue to do the most incredible stuff to my flesh.

"Yeah, yeah, yeah, yeah, yeah, yeah, yeah, yeah My Dirty Bear, you adore it. "And I love all three Bears. Now you're my Gentle Bear, sometimes you're my Sexy Bear, and sometimes you're my very Dirty Bear." "I'm sorry, I'm not a blond," she chuckled.

"I adore you just as you are, Goldilocks."

Diana stood back and kissed my heaving chest and neck, which were sticky and salty with sweat. When I regained my strength, I cradled her in my arms, my little love fitting like we were cut from the same block of marble, our legs entwined, and our bodies melded. We interacted solely by touch; we didn't need to say "I love you" at the time. It just flowed between us.

After some cuddling, we took a shower, dressed, and Diana drove me into Cold Spring. We walked around a little while when we decided to go to a local deli and get some sandwiches and drinks and took it to the town park, spread out my ever-present blanket, and we had a kind of picnic. "Angel, this is ideal. Being around you is ideal. I work hard, but I still get distracted by thoughts of you several times a day. What you're doing, how much more fun you're having, and with whom you have it." I looked down, embarrassed by my vulnerability.

"Bear, you know the last thing you need to be concerned about is me meeting someone else. I'm so in love with you that I don't think of the other guys as anything other than coworkers or friends. Some of them are very good-looking, I admit. But none are nearly in your league, not as far as I'm concerned." She set her sandwich down and leaned against me, hugging me close. She swept my bushy hair away from my brow. "I'm not interested in anything else, Jon." It's not enticing. When I'm feeling sad at night, I still think about you. Nobody else crosses my mind. Jon, I adore you. You are the only one." She kissed me, not a little, cute kiss, but a big, wet kiss, unconcerned with who was passing by or watching us. It was one of the most loving kisses we'd ever shared.

"How did I come across you?" I'm extremely fortunate. "I met my soul friend."

"Because Elizabeth outperformed me for valedictorian. We might not be here today if I hadn't come in first."

"I disapprove. Some stuff, I believe, is predestined. Diana, I believe we were supposed to meet. We would have had to wait a couple more weeks, but we were doomed. At least, that's what I'd like to believe. And, despite how horny I am, I haven't touched myself because you've been gone. But I never consider another lady. You are the only survivor."

"Bear, I wish you'd touch yourself. When you're home in the middle of the night, and consider some naughty, even filthy, fantasies you might have about me. One of them may as well be having fun." She slipped her hand under my t-shirt and hugged my stomach and chest, which was fantastic.

"Would you want me to?" "Jerk off, were you dreaming about me?"

"Who else do I want you to consider?" She questioned, with a 'Duh' look on her face. I grinned, slightly embarrassed.

"That's right. I'll do it in a couple of nights and tell you more about it the next time we meet."

Diana smiled her soft and gentle chuckle, which I adored. We consumed our lunch gently, always touching intimately but not in a manner that might land us in jail (haha). We walked even more after that, arms around each other. We walked into a music shop and looked at the albums, discussing albums we had or wished to buy. I purchased Elvis Costello's Armed Forces and Joni Mitchell's 1971 album Blue for Diana while I had to carry it home with me.

"You weren't required to do that, Bear. I might afford to purchase my albums."

"I understand, my love. I just needed to. It's a fantastic record. That reminds me of something. My roommate notification arrived yesterday. I have to contact him tomorrow. Steve...shit, I can't recall his name right now. He resides in Syosset (Long Island). "We can see whether we'll get together or destroy each other," I joked, "but most importantly, we can organize what we're carrying." I want to bring my stereo; he should bring a TV if that's more convenient for him. You can have mine this week as well."

"I'll contact my parents tomorrow and see if the letter was sent to me." This is terrifying. You can just expect to meet somebody you get along with. I just wish we could have shared a bed." That sounded wonderful to me, so I drew her close. "Bear, take me back to my place." I need to have some fun with you. This time it's nice and slow."

I kissed her on the top of her head, then on her mouth. "Angel, there's nothing I'd ever get. Too long as it's just you and you alone." Diana was gripping my right arm and kissing my shoulder as I drove back to the hotel. We went inside, and instead of removing our clothes, we stood in front of each other and took turns undressing each other. Diana took the lead, gently pulling my top above my head and licking my chest, including my nipples. I moaned quietly, my fingertips stroking through her fine, silky hair. She unbuckled my belt and undid my jeans, slipping them off slowly as she did my top. Diana also assisted me in removing my shoes and socks before removing my briefs.

"You look scrumptious, my sexy Bear." But first and foremost, it's my time." Her voice had the enthusiastic tone that I recognized because I was feeling the same way.

"I can hardly wait to strip you bare, Angel." But I'll do it. "I'm trying to take it about as slowly as you did." I kissed her a few quick loving kisses before steadily bringing her tie-dyed top-up, then tossed her bra aside. I kissed her throat and her body, and she rubbed my shoulders with moans of her own. I knelt in front of her and supported her with her ankle socks and sneakers. And

106

there was her underwear, plain blue, nothing overtly suggestive, but she looked unbelievably sexy in them. Diana was sexy no matter what she wore or didn't wear, in my opinion. To me, it's simply stunning.

I stayed on my knees and kissed her lower tummy. Her skin trembled with enthusiasm, and she clutched my head for support on her feet. Then she ran her fingertips through my sandy hair in a sensual way.

Diana spread her feet about a foot apart so my tongue could sample and taunt her. Her hips swiveled slightly as she giggled, causing me to follow her. But, just when my tongue was about to sample her delicious nectar, Diana softly pulled my head back and whispered, "No, my Bear. I told you I wanted to have sexual relations with you. And lie down for me. Simply settle down."

"I'd do anything for you, Angel." I stood up and kissed her before lying down on the bed on my back. Diana walked steadily as the shadows through the window rose, illuminating her face and body with overlapping stripes of orange and shadow from the blinds. Diana relaxed her body while remaining upright, straddling me on her feet; our palms joined tightly as our bodies rocked softly in sync.

"Jon, I love this," she said, moving her hands casually. "I have a lot of feelings about you. I usually do, but not right now..." As an orgasm flowed through her body, she screamed and gritted her teeth.

"I understand, honey. "I see that as well." My legs were swaying back and forth to rub on her clit to keep her orgasm moving. "I'm madly in love with you, Angel. "I feel like I'll be in love with you forever."

"You're such a nice and romantic person. It's a bit mushy. It's fantastic. I adore you just as you are, my huge Bear. Often he's gentle and friendly, and other times he's hard and manly. "Always the correct one at the right moment."

I began to sit up straight and assisted Diana in adjusting her legs to go straight past my back, then around me, and my legs remained straight. We were sitting up, facing each other, arms and legs outstretched. We were all connected by our genitals and rocked back and forth together. Touching and kissing, sweet and caring. We were able to avoid traveling too far, allowing us to enjoy this fantastic experience for as long as possible. We were almost absolutely together.

Our breathing was slow and steady, and we were starting to feel sweaty again. Suddenly, without notice, Diana's orgasm rose and nearly erupted in her bones, and then the same thing happened to me when my sperm splashed inside her, and we both shook with excitement. We kept kissing, our tongues roaming over each other's mouths, arms, and chests. We stayed seated like that by gripping each other closely.

"Thank you so much, Angel. That was the case... "I can't quite come up with a name for it."

"You'll never need to repay me for expressing my affection with you." But I agree; there are no words to describe how amazing that was. "You are my life's passion."

"How come you have too many other people to equate me to?" With a chuckle and a kiss, I said.

"Hundreds of thousands." Didn't you remember you're just the next in a long line of men I've had feelings for?" Diana said with a huge, sly grin.

We were going rigid like that, and sitting with no lower help was hurting my back. We carefully untangled ourselves before taking turns in the shower. It was almost 6 p.m. by then, and we needed to have another shower together, our third of the day.

"I hope no one smells my shampoo later," Diana joked. "And I believe my skin is raw. I believe it's my vagina. So it doesn't bother me. Just don't let me sprint!"

"Yes, I believe my penis has red spots. But it was well worth it, my dear. I'm already looking forward to seeing you next week."

Diana's amusement had subsided. "Bear, you won't see me next week. I decided to offer up my day to have the two days for the concert the next week. Please accept my apologies, my affection. It was the only choice."

For a moment, I stood, depressed. "If you wanted to, you had to, honey. We'll be taking two days off together. Tuesday night, before I drive you back up here, you should visit our families for an hour or two. We're going to make a deal. Overall, I believe we can come out ahead. Consider how much we'll miss each other by then. We'll make it a memorable evening. I'll book our space at a good hotel in town. It will save you time after the show...and before it as well."

"You have such a beautifully filthy mind, my love," Diana said as she sat across my lap in her underwear. "However, the next time we do this, I'm wearing extra socks!" We had a lot of laughs and kisses together. I'm not sure how many kisses we exchanged that day, but it had to be at least three hundred—even a lot more. We couldn't hold our mouths shut.

We changed into our clothes and signed out. We still had about two hours until Diana returned, so we stopped for dinner at a tiny cafe in town. She couldn't consume wine, but we drank soft drinks with our pasta dinners and tried not to worry about having to split again that night. We only walked after dinner when twilight turned to darkness. The town was quite cool, with various kitsch and vintage shops, various bars and restaurants, and the types of stores that residents wanted daily, such as a bakery and other shops. It was (is) a rather upscale town on the Hudson River's Eastside, a few miles north of West Point on the opposite bank.

We spent our last hour sitting by the water, watching boats and ships move up and down the river, now low dark mountains on the other side, and some houses lit up. It was serene and lovely. We stared into each other's eyes, a combination of excitement and sorrow in our eyes. We didn't say anything because it was difficult to find sentences. We had to get moving after a bit. It stung like hell.

We arrived at the parking lot around 8:30 a.m., with plenty of time until she had to be with her girls. We went into the office, and whoever took over for Lenny at the desk gave Diana permission to carry me into the grounds before 9:30, when they had to start having the kids ready for bed. She led me back to the dining area, where there were several nighttime games with music going on. She introduced me to a few people, including one or two guys who wished they were in my role, but everybody was kind. Diana excused herself for a couple of moments to find her group, and then she took them back to see me again. It was enjoyable conversing with them, and when Diana had to lead me back to the parking lot, a couple of the girls created ooohing and ahhing noises and kissing sounds. Diana smiled brightly, and I waved goodnight to everybody.

A few last kisses in my seat. "Angel, I miss you terribly, so I'm happy you're doing this. Those children adore you. I'm sorry I didn't take your advice; I should have done the same. I'd have less income, but I'd have a fantastic summer."

"Bear, next season. There will already be next year." We kissed one last time, long, short, and sad. She got out of the vehicle, tears streaming down her cheeks, and leaned against my window. "Jon, you drive safely home. Thursday night, I'll contact you. Also, please inform Cammy that I will email her this week. I adore you to the moon and beyond."

I, too, was moved to tears. "I intend to be cautious. I'll talk to you on Thursday. Honey, I already miss you."

"Oh no, now I'm going to sob in front of everybody! You'd best go before I pull you back into my space and bind you up!" She kissed me quickly and hurried forward, so we didn't linger for longer. It was already after 9:30 p.m., and I had a long ride home.

I arrived home in an hour and ten minutes, so I was home until 11 p.m. Cammy was still in bed; her camp bus picked her up at 8 a.m. every morning, she had long, busy days, and she was having a wonderful summer. I went into my parents' space and spoke to them for a bit, offering them the gist of my day without getting into specifics. I was tired at that point, so I said goodnight, did what I needed to do, and fell asleep within minutes of laying down. Yet I was also saddened by the fact that I wouldn't be seeing Diana for the next two weeks.

XXXXXXXXXXXXXXXXXXXXXXXXXXXXXXXXXXXXXXXXXXX
XXXXXXXXXXXXXXXXXXXXXXXXXXXXXXXXXXXXXXXXXXX
XXXXXXXXXXXXXXXXXXXXXX

The next two weeks were much more difficult than the two weeks before Diana and I met for the first time. I held myself occupied most nights by attending a few Dr. Pepper Music Festival gigs in Central Park, America, one night and The Tubes the next (If you've never seen or heard of the Tubes, look them up on YouTube). They're unfathomable). Five dollars for a ticket was a steal right back then. Cammy and I went to Mets and Yankees games with our father. About how much fun these events were, I missed Diana more than words could express. It wasn't the lack of sex, though we both missed it. It had to be her. All about her is fine. Her company and our closeness.

When Diana had the opportunity, we spoke several times. Cammy sent a letter at the end of the week, which brightened her day (she didn't share with me!). and I received one the same day. It wasn't that much, and she didn't have time for that. However, there was a lot of love in every section, every phrase. It moved my heart and making me feel bad for not writing to her. So, after reading the three pages three times, I sat down at my desk and sent her my post. It was a little longer (I had more time), and it was packed with my passion and heartbreak over losing her.

After seeing Diana, I contacted Steven Lindt, my soon-to-be college roommate, over the weekend. He seemed to be a nice person. We spoke about some general topics and got along; we decided that I would bring my stereo system and he would bring a black and white television, but we weren't going to see it much other than sports and news. Then the topic of females came up. I told him that I had a girlfriend and that we were madly in love. He practically told me that he considered himself a lady's man and expected to be out of our space several times but that he would like to have the room himself now and again. I said that I was certain we should agree. So my outlook seemed to be quite promising.

Diana's case was more complex. Robin, her roommate, came from a tiny town in upstate New York near Lake Placid, not far from the Canadian frontier. And she was a devout Born Again Christian with a vague understanding of what she considered 'sin.' Such as alcohol and premarital intercourse. Like in rock music. If she went home on weekends, Robin wouldn't be spending many nights away from her room. However, it was just as far away from Binghamton as Queens, a four-hour drive in either direction. Diana was concerned about just getting along with her.

Finally, Monday, the 23rd, and I were up and out of the house much faster than normal, hoping to avoid any traffic. I arrived at 8:30 a.m., a little early, and this time there was a young woman at the counter, Margie. She had anticipated my arrival, although a little later. She asked if I knew where the dining hall was, and when I said I did, she offered me a guest tag for my shirt (of course, a Grateful Dead shirt!) and informed me I should go there myself. That was another epoch.

When I arrived at the dining hall, I searched the huge space for Diana. She was the first to recognize me and waved from the center of the packed space. I ran up to her, and she stood up and embraced and kissed me like we'd known each other for a year, not two weeks. All erupted in good-natured catcalls and cheers, and I doubt we would have minded anyway. We hugged each other for at least a minute until her party cleared a seat at the table for me. Diana requested a tray of pancakes and turkey sausage from one of the waiters. I was thankful because I was starving and consumed as much as I could. Diana's children laughed as they watched me feed as I'd never seen food before, and she even got me a second serving. I let out a belly laugh, which made the kids and a couple of other counselors laugh. "Girls, stay away; he's all mine!" Diana burst out laughing, and there were more laughs at my expense. It was fine because it was entertaining and humorous.

When I was done, Diana kissed each of her girls and informed them to behave for her assistants and that she'd see them the next night. She was a true mother hen to them, not because it was her work, but because she cared about them. It came from her enormous heart. There was enough room in there for her to enjoy her dad, me, and her campers. It was also another aspect of her that I admired.

We placed her overnight bag in my trunk, got in my car, drove down the road a little, and I pulled over to say hello properly. We hugged and held each other for at least five minutes before saying our I love yous. She looked at my shirt and said, "You're wearing a Dead shirt! We'll need to find one for me before we leave tonight."

"Did you expect to go to the concert without a shirt? Angel, you're a moron." I turned around and pulled a gift bag from the back seat, which I gave to her. Diana squealed with joy as she picked out a Dancing Bears tie-dyed tee in her size and wrapped her arms around me, kissing me all over.

"You're the greatest! I can't believe you went out of your way to help me!"

"I didn't get you a diamond ring, honey. It's just a shirt."

"It's not a shirt!' It's very kind of you to think of it for me. You're a hot, sweet man,"...a kiss on my nose..." Another kiss on my mouth, broad and soft and with a promise of what was to come.

There wasn't much traffic on the lane, so Diana changed her shirt as fast as a rabbit for the one I bought her in less than twenty seconds. Except her top was brand new; she resembled any other concert-going Dead Head. She was absolutely cute.
I returned to the city, and since it was already early (check-in time at the hotel was after 2 p.m.), we returned home. This is my house. Cammy was away at camp, and my parents were at work. I parked across the street, and much as the last time, our clothes

began falling off as soon as we walked in the driveway, but this time the door in question was my bedroom door. We were rolling on top of each other some twenty seconds after we were naked. Our bodies were aroused and wet, and our kisses and touches were improving the situation. We were so in love, but Diana prevented me. "I want to look after you, my sexy Bear."
"You're not obligated to do anything with me, Angel. We're all in this together to make each other proud."

"Don't worry; you'll make amends to me." So I'll go first. You make those long drives to see me by yourself, you buy the seats, and you get me the cool jersey. You've been wonderful to me in a thousand respects.

Finally, I must cum. I could sense her lovely sexual fragrance filling the space, so I knew she was hot. We were standing next to the bunk, and Diana was hunched down, her arms resting on the corner of the mattress. I was beating on her from behind, both of us grunting loudly, both of us on the verge of a smashing orgasm. I drew her upper body back towards me, kissing her neck as she let out small, fast gasps with each thrust. This time it reached me first, and I was spraying her damp tunnel with my sticky cream. Diana sensed it as well, and we all became silent except for our breathing. We weren't doing something illegal, but...who was home so early in the afternoon?

118

We sat silently on my bunk, only listening before I heard my father's voice...and the voice of a woman who was not my mother. They were laughing together, very sweet, almost intimately. I understood just what it sounded like. I saw it firsthand. My stomach was twisting with a fiery knot. Diana had wide eyes and was looking at me with concern as I glanced at her. She was as upset as I was.

I sprung to my feet and threw on my panties before slipping into my cutoff jean shorts. "What are you doing, Jon?" She hissed as quietly as she possibly could.

"I'm going down there to prevent my father from messing around on my girlfriend, nothing else."

"Jon, love, just worry about this." We could hear them in the living room, their laughter fading into a sexual rhythm we'd seen before. He's a jerk. He's a jerk. "You'll insult the four of us if you confront him now." It's best if you take him off guard and speak to him alone."

"He's about to cheat on my mother, Diana!" I will put a halt to him right now! What if it's their first moment or his first time? I could prevent him from having an affair with my mother! Don't you think it's worthwhile? I may shame us. However, I will save my mother from the most humiliating kind of embarrassment.

Besides, do you suppose we can wait up here in silence for however long it takes to hear them screw? That's what I can't do. "Do you think you can?" She shook her head no, a depressed look on her face. "Please accept my apologies, honey." This is everything I would do. I have to give it a shot."

Diana rolled out of bed, putting on her clothing with a painfully depressing look on her lips. "At the very least, let me accompany you. I will assist you, and maybe it would benefit the woman in any way." Her hand met mine, and we gripped each other tightly. I quickly kissed her and then went to my house.

I didn't open it softly because I needed him to understand me, and he did. I saw him seem like one of the moles in an amusement park's Whack-a-Mole novelty games. Such fuzzy animals were adorable, but there was nothing adorable about my father or the look on his face when he turned to the top of the stairs, where my space was.

"Who is Jon?" "What are you doing at home?" I saw some legs, cool long stockinged legs, running along with the sofa.

"I should have asked you that." "How come you're not at work?" I was already at the top of the stairs, staring down at him, which gave me an edge psychologically. Diana was not the only one who enjoyed reading about psychology. She emerged from my space and took a seat by my side at the railing.

My father worked out what was going on, but he couldn't use that to his benefit because Diana and I weren't doing something illegal, except in a religious way. On the other side, he was unquestionably in error.

"Hello, Diana," he said hesitantly.

"Good day, Mr. Grossman." Her speech was as hard as a stone.

"Hello, Diana. It's Al." "I told you months earlier."

"Indeed, Mr. Grossman." She wasn't going to give an inch.

At that stage, the other lady stood. Without a doubt, she was a beauty, tall with short red hair, a killer physique, and a reasonably sweet smile. I didn't mind. She was assisting him in cheating on my mother.

"I...um...I suppose I should get going." She collected her belongings and slunk down the hall to the bathroom to get ready. That shook me to my heart. The inference was that she had already visited our home. Was it at a gathering? I will have most definitely seen her. Or does it imply that this wasn't the first time he'd done anything like this for her?

I took my time descending the steps. In a shaking fury, I stepped in front of him and yelled, "You son of a bitch."

"I'm still your dad!" That's not how you refer to me!"

"Dad, you always told me that appreciation does not come naturally. It's well deserved. You've lost a lot of confidence today. Don't worry; I'm not going to say, Mom. No, not yet. I couldn't do it to her. Yet I can't look you in the eyes right now. Return to your job. And don't even think about bringing a lady back here to mess around again. I'll mention anything if I figure out you did that. "Believe me."

"What were you doing here, Mr. High and Mighty?" "Are you two holding hands?" My father was angry with me for speaking to him in this manner. Furious didn't even begin to explain how I felt about him at the time.

"I came here with my girlfriend, whom I adore." You can't mean the same thing. In the very least, you could not claim the same." I stormed upstairs with Diana, entered my place, and slammed the door behind me. I couldn't say anything more about him.

We took a seat at the foot of my bunk. I was experiencing a range of negative feelings. Rage, betrayal, deep sadness, and depression would be difficult enough to meet my father, but how could I look at my mother and hide this terrible secret from her? Diana's arm was wrapped around my back, gently stroking my neck and shoulder, but I was so stiff. She drew me back so we could lie on the bunk. I cried as she flipped me around to face her, her fingernails tracing down my cheeks as she looked into my eyes with her lovely blue eyes. I sobbed. There was a flood of tears. I felt as if I were inconsolable. I wrapped my arms around Diana, and she continued to kiss my head, run her fingertips through my hair, and pin my face to her breast behind her shirt. "Let it all hang out, Bear." My gentle and warm devotion. I'm here to help you. I'll be there with you at all times."

Thank goodness she was with me when this occurred. I still don't know if I should have held things intact otherwise. The agony was intense and widespread. But Diana, my true Angel, was offering me the power to endure it, at least for the time being.

"Thank you so much, honey. You seem to be protecting my sanity. In a million years, I would never have thought he could do it. I'm not sure if I'm going to deal with him. How would I possibly deceive my mother? What am I going to do, Diana? We have six weeks before we start training."

"Dear Sweetheart, I'm not sure. I'm afraid I don't have any responses for you."

"Oh my Goodness, Cammy!" I can't tell my mother! It would hinder Diana so that it would destroy Cammy. Aside from her Brother's Little Sister, she is Daddy's girl. She'll be killed once she discovers who her father is..." I jumped up and dashed to the restroom, arriving just in time to vomit the rest of my big meal. Diana didn't sit down, instead of entering the bathroom and stroking her palm up and down my back. When I finished heaving, I flushed and sat against the tiled wall, crying again, this time only a profound sorrow fleeing my soul. She approached me and rested her head on my back from the edge.

"I apologize, Angel. This is destroying our day. We should have a fantastic time. It's a shambles."

"Bear, look at me," she said commandingly. Diana was tough when she wanted to be. I fixed my gaze on her and prepared to listen. However, first... "Wait, clean your teeth first. Sorry, but your breath stinks..." I gave a small grin and went to the sink to brush my teeth thoroughly, followed by mouthwash.

"All right, better?" As I sat next to her again, I inquired.

"Much," Diana said with a grin, gently kissing me to highlight how clean my breath was. "OK, well. First and foremost, you have little to apologize for. Your father does, but he should apologize to you and particularly to your mother. I don't think whether we go to the concert or not right now. There will be many chances for both Dead and other artists to perform. What I am concerned about is what is right for you and us. If that's what you like, I'm comfortable with only having each other all night. "All I want to do tonight is be there for you."

I kissed Diana and hugged her close. "I'd like to go tonight. I realize you've been anticipating this performance for weeks. I've done the same. I'm not going to make him destroy this for us. I have to drive you back to camp tomorrow night, and then I have to come home and deal with him. Paul Grossman is an accountant, a family man, and a cheater. But today, tonight, and tomorrow, I want to spend time with the most incredible woman I meet. My adoration. My whole being." We embraced there on the bathroom tile, still seated. I was holding her, relieved a lot of pain. At least for the day.

We gathered ourselves together and left my place. Surprisingly, we were still starving, so we went to our nearest Kosher deli and shared some hot dogs and a potato knish, as well as a pair of Dr. Brown's Diet sodas, Cream for Diana, and Black Cherry for me. (Trust me, they're the finest diet soft drinks you'll find anywhere!) Then we went into Manhattan and checked into our

125

hotel, The Hilton on 6th and 54th, just a few blocks from Radio City Music Hall.

The remainder of the day was spent lying in bed and making love. We loved each other, which I believe was what we wanted to feel like ourselves. Diana resurrected the part of me that made me feel normal once more.

We walked the few blocks to Radio City at 6 p.m., and there was already a crowd of Dead Heads and want tobes (like Diana and me) milling around outside, two hours before the broadcast. Many young people wandered about with a single finger in the air (indicating that they just wanted one fare), and posters read 'I NEED A MIRACLE!', asking for a ticket, preferably for free. We moved a few more blocks to a coffee shop and bought something light to eat. We also had good appetites, even though we were both 18 and competitive. And we headed back in as the doors opened at 7:30 a.m.

It's a stunning Art Deco theatre from the 1930s that seats around 6,000 people and has excellent music. It's an excellent venue for a gig. We took seats at the front of the first balcony.

"Thank you so much, Bear. My very first Dead show!" Diana was thrilled, and I was overjoyed for her. Plus, I liked going to gigs, and I grew to appreciate the Grateful Dead more and more each year. Many of you who are fans will recognize what I'm referring to. Being there, particularly with Diana, was a welcome diversion.

The lights went out just after 8 p.m., and the band emerged, tuning their guitars and breaking out into Bertha, one of their favourite openers. Everyone was on their feet, even Diana, jumping at their seats and in the aisles, others high on ecstasy. When the scent of marijuana filled the house, I lit one of the three joints I had brought, puffed, and handed it to Diana. She sent me a questioning glance before taking a puff and coughing her ass off. She handed it back to me, and I struck it again, passing it on as other joints passed by. Diana took another drag before waving it off, and I was happily buzzed. It wasn't for her, but she didn't mind if I joined in.

Before taking a break, Jerry, Bob, and the guys (and Donna Jean) performed several well-known songs such as Cassidy, Row Jimmy, Deal, and Peggy-O. We stayed for a bit after the lights came on.

"They're amazing!" exclaimed my new Dead Head girlfriend as she kissed me on the lips. "I'm having a fantastic time! Except for the smoke, of course. My throat is parched. Could you please bring us anything to drink?"

"Angel, of course. You are welcome to wait here. I won't be gone far." We kissed once more, and I went to get us a fountain drink from the concession stand, packed with thirsty and hungry people. Diana gratefully sipped a long draw from the straw while I took back a big Coke with lots of colds. The second set was almost as entertaining. Dire Wolf, Fire on the Mountain, Scarlet Begonias, and Terrapin Station, all with lengthy jams, I Know You Rider, China Cat Sunflower, and a fantastic Sunshine Daydream and Stuck Inside of Mobile... finale 2 The lights came up. We filed out, a cloud of smoke lingering in the background, stinging our eyes and throats, but it didn't bother us. It was a fantastic exhibition and a fantastic time.

I placed my arm around Diana and said as we steadily made our way to the aisle stairs, "So, what do you think? Was the second collection on par with the first?"

"Much better! Except for the smoke, of course. I can't wait to get some fresh air outdoors. But, Bear, this was a fantastic moment. Thank you so much for getting me here." We wrapped our arms around each other and led the crowd before we got outside. It was a nice four-block walk to our hotel on a warm yet cool night. It also made it easy for us to relax and made our eyes feel brighter. It was late in several ways, but Midtown Manhattan never sleeps, and there was plenty of traffic with associated noises on our tour. I adored Manhattan and wished that one day I would be able to move there.

When we returned to our place, I filled a bucket of ice from the machine down the hall, and we drank from the mini-bar. We undressed, changed into some light sleepwear, and cuddled whilst watching some television. "Diana, do you mind if we just chill like this for a bit and then go to bed? I'm exhausted; it's been a busy day. And not everyone has been enjoyable."

"Jon, I'm so happy you brought it up. I believe I am still overtired. I just want to sleep next to you while holding my huge sweet Bear. We'll make up for it in the morning, right? "She inquired, optimistic.

"It will be fantastic. It's a fantastic way to start the day. particularly in your case." We kissed a couple of times and switched off the lights, keeping the television on as we cuddled. "My Angel, I adore you. Thank you for putting up with me this afternoon."

"Bear, you'll never have to thank me for that. That's why we're here: to support each other. I adore you. Almost always." She made a contented sound as she snuggled up to me. I was more concerned with my parents than I was about Diana. I had little idea how I would approach my father or even my mother without spilling the beans. Damn him for destroying our family. Diana fell asleep instantly, but it took me a long time to fall asleep.

Diana Love Story (PT. 4)

We go to work, and our bond becomes stronger.

Tina Scott

Diana bounded awake when the alarm went off at 9, but I failed to get there. I'd had a lot less sleep, and it was showing. We produced the little free pot of coffee in the room and sipped it while sitting in bed after taking turns in the shower. "You don't look like you got much sleep, sweetheart," she noted. "I'm pretty sure I knew why."

"Yes, something came back to us when we were lying here. What am I going to do with my father? What about my family? My mother will be crushed if she finds out. Camilla would be crushed as a result. I'm at a loss as to how to cope with this. I honestly don't."

"I'm going to suggest Bear. And bear with me. What do you think of spending the remainder of the summer with me at camp? It can hold you away from your home until your emotions have calmed down. Even with nearly five weeks to go, they could still use a few counselors, especially for two of the boy's classes. I believe it would be better for you."

"What about my responsibilities to Sy and Marilyn? What about Camilla and my mother? Cammy will think something is wrong, and Mom will suspect something is wrong. I told her that I would do stuff for her. She'll be seriously injured. I'd consider it if we weren't starting school a week after camp ended. I'm most concerned with Cammy. If it should fall out, she'll be right in the center of it."

"I'm still concerned for you, Jon. If it doesn't fall out, you and your father will be arguing before you leave for kindergarten. You will be enraged because it will poison you. And it can contaminate all of the marriages, including ours. Whatever you decide, I'll be there for you. But, please, think about it. And I've got an idea. We clean up, sign out, get a bite to eat, and head back to camp. You could try out one of the groups for the day and see if you like it. If you wish to do so, they will enable you to begin next week to end the week at the printers. I believe you need this, sweetheart. Home isn't going to save you right now."

I considered it. It seemed like just what I was looking for. Mom would understand, but she would be disappointed. Camilla, on the other hand, will be wounded. That isn't good. Still, I had to prioritize my desires. I thought I'd give it a shot. Maybe I won't like it, and the point is moot. "OK, I'll give it a shot. We should probably have some cleaning done."

We also took a shower at the same time. We took turns soaping each other up after shampooing my hair (we didn't have time to do Diana's long hair), and touching leads to hugging, and kissing led to more touching and more aggressiveness. Meanwhile, I steered her, so she was sitting against the white tiles, and we kissed under the steaming hot water.

"My sexy Angel," I exclaimed as Diana moved her hand quicker, then slower, alternating her grasp and action in no discernible pattern. It was both exhilarating and stressful because I couldn't fall into a groove. "Do you realize you're making me insane?"

"Maybe I might focus more if your fingertips weren't doing magical stuff to my body. But don't even think about doing what you're doing!" Diana's hips pressed down tightly on my fingertips a minute later, and I pinched her clit as she approached, her lips caressing mine. "That was intense! You have such potential! "With a chuckle, she said. "It's now your time. Let's get you out of here." "You're so sweet to me," I exclaimed, catching my breath. Diana had her hair in a shower cap, but she always looked stunning to me, and I promised myself that if we lived the next 70 years together, she would remain so.

We dried off and did the stuff we needed to do to prepare for the day after some more soaping up to wash my sperm off Diana.

We checked out, retrieved my car from the ridiculously overpriced parking space, and drove through Manhattan traffic into Queens. We stopped at a diner for breakfast (including REAL bacon!) before heading back to the camp.

We were relatively silent on the way upstate. We listened to music on my eight-track and sang along a bit, but my mind was elsewhere. The loss to my family was something I kept circling in my mind. I understood what I wanted to do when we came within a few miles of the camp. I wanted to get home. I wanted to be truthful with Diana. Diana didn't say anything when I sped by the center; I looked at her and saw she understood what was coming. We stopped at a nearby deli for a drink and relaxed in the same park where we had lunch a few weeks before.

"That's fine, Jon. Tell me what I already remember."

"I have to go home, honey; it has nothing to do with my career. It's a member of my kin. I know my father, and I may have difficult times, but I can't leave them like this. Mom and Cammy have no idea what's going on, and I realize my issue with my father would make it difficult, and they'll ask what's going on. So they'd be suspicious if I just left my work and flew to here. Because if anything falls out when I'm gone, they'll be devastated because I won't be around to assist them. What if I make this work and my mother finds out after two weeks? I'd have to quit right after I got started. This whole thing is totally messed up."

"I suppose there's nothing I can suggest to persuade you otherwise, is there?" No, I said, shaking my head. There wasn't any. Diana let out a deep breath of sorrow and disappointment. "I don't want you to get hurt. Or your loved ones. Or it might be us. I wish you could all forget what we saw and go on about your life as if nothing had changed, but that's not true."

"No, Angel. It isn't. I don't believe anybody would ever forget it. It's pretty much ingrained in my mind." Diana slid closer to me on the park bench, and we hugged closely. We were silent for a moment, and a couple of her campmates came nearby, even on their day off. They began to approach, but Diana shook her head back and forth, signaling them to stay clear. "Thank you for having them feel it wasn't a nice time, honey."

"That's not a challenge, Bear. It's a very bad moment right now. If you're curious, I'm terrified shit. We're worried about how much this would cost us. The last thing I expect to happen is for you to leave me. I'm sure you'll be so hurt that it would affect those around you."

"I think I can't promise that won't happen. What I can claim is that I adore you and require your presence in my life. You might be the thing that saves my season. I'll see you once a week. And though it's just to drive in my car all day and hold each other. Next week, I'll be here."

She was shedding a few tears, nothing major, but Diana was sad, sad for me. Hell, I was down as well. She said, "Why don't you join me at camp for the rest of the day? Sheryl, the camp owner, will let you spend the rest of the day with us and linger for dinner. So long as we don't get too sentimental." Her grin melted my aching heart as she looked back at me.

"Sure, if you're sure, let's go. I'll look at how my girlfriend spends her time away from me." We kissed a couple of times before walking to my car and driving to camp.

Sure enough, the owner, a lovely lady called Sheryl, permitted me to remain until 9 p.m. as long as I remained with Diana's party. It was about 2 p.m., so there was plenty of time, particularly because dinner was served at 6 p.m. Since I didn't have a bathing suit, the one thing I couldn't do was float.

It was a great pleasure. Her party was delighted to see Diana return early, and the girls were overjoyed to have a 'child' counselor for a few hours. We played softball (some of those kids were very good), I remained with the senior workers while the rest of the camp went swimming in the afternoon, and then I entered the squad for an Arts & Crafts activity before dinner. I stuck with Diana and her friends the whole time, resisting the temptation to embrace her and sneaking in a couple of moments of hand-holding. Aside from Diana, the girls argued for who will sit next to me. They were lovely children. They made me think of my sister, who reminded me why I wanted to be at home. Cammy might need my assistance.

Following dinner, there was a large fire, chanting, and toasting marshmallows about what you'd find at a campfire at night. Diana instructed her girls to say farewell to me at 8 p.m. and told her assistants she'd be back in an hour. Cynthia grinned knowingly, recognizing that because it was officially her day off, she might take an hour. I said goodnight to everybody, and they all said it back, with a few staff members blowing whistles and creating other noises.

Diana said as we walked to my vehicle, "Drive around a quarter-mile to the side road on the right. We'll get some peace for a bit." I understood what she was thinking, and it succeeded for me as well. I exited the main road and entered a side road, where I discovered a tiny clearing. It's fine. "We don't have much time, so hurry up. Let's take the back seat."

"Yes, ma'am," I replied, mock saluting her. We dashed into the back room and were embracing and touching each other in no time. My hand slipped under Diana's top and bra, cupping her right breast and lightly pulling on her nipple. She moaned in my mouth while rubbing my chest beneath my sweater, her slender fingers raking through my hairs. Our shirts and bras were then off, and I assisted her in lying back on the seat as I sucked her left nipple with hunger.

"It feels so sweet, Bear," she said as I helped her out of her cut-off shorts and pantyhose. After that, Diana caught my head and pulled my lips to hers for a slew of hot, smoking-hot kisses. "Jon, I need you to fuck me. Don't want to make love to me. Fuck me like it's our last night alive. Do it ferociously, like my Dirty Bear."

"Honey, don't worry, we're not breaking..."
"Yes, yes, yes, yes, yes, yes, yes, yes, yes, yes This is what I want of you tonight. I want you to cum me over and over again. So I'll make certain you blow up for me. But, please, take me seriously tonight!" Her voice almost begged me, and to be fair, I wanted her just as much.
"If that's what you're looking for, my Naughty Devil." I kissed her passionately. Diana gasped out, her back arched, and she put her feet down on the seat to reach me halfway, a great match. Her legs wrapped around my waist, her arms wrapped around my upper back, and we repeatedly kissed as I thrust deep and heavy. And, through Diana's tightness, I was able to

139

shift freely inside her with a perfectly normal motion. We were so in sync with each other by then.

Our gestures were similar to those of skilled performers at the time.

Our moves, though, were far from the elegance synonymous with experienced performers. We were fucking each other like beasts, with grunts and cries that can be associated with raw physical touch. Diana scraped her nails down my back, and my balls slapped loudly against her rear. I pulled firmly and ground my pubic bone on her clit every five to six strokes, and she would scream out and shudder, even to a full orgasm. Then we began again, fucking a little faster, and then she came back, maybe ten minutes later.

"Do you think you'll be able to cum with me the next time, Bear?" Diana inquired, smiling up at me and exhaling heavily.

"I'll give it a shot, honey. I'd be delighted to." I kissed her softer, then let myself go, figuring out my own pace for orgasm. We were thrusting with each other, raping each other with the intention of a mutual orgasm. Her hands squeezed my butt cheeks, her nails digging in slightly, exhilarating me evermore. We were sweaty, we were out of steam, and we were ecstatic for each other. Our tongues keep meeting each other, kissing all over our mouths, necks, and backs.

We wished we could spend the night together, even though it meant sleeping in the back seat of my vehicle. But it couldn't happen; she needed to go back to her campers, and I needed to get home, no matter how exhausted I was. The very last thing I needed to do was confront my father. Not that night, and certainly not anytime soon. So I didn't have a say. I needed to get to work the following day.

Diana and I hugged each other, unable to bear the thought of the night coming to an end. "I have to get ready, Bear. I have to go. I'm sorry I did. Furthermore, you must get on the path before it is too late. And do me a favor and get a Coke or Pepsi from the grocery shop. Anything caffeinated to get you home."

"Yes, I'll be up all night. Don't be concerned for me, Angel. I'm going to be great. I'll listen to the radio or a cassette and sing along. Besides, if I don't make the music, I'll have a lot on my mind. I'm not going to doze off while driving. Can you contact me on Thursday night?"

"As is customary. You couldn't put an end to me." We'd moved to the front so I could drop her off at the office. I arrived a few minutes before 9 a.m., and we kept hands every second before the clock struck 9 a.m. "My tall, precious Bear, I adore you. Please drive with caution. Make me a promise!"

"Angel, I swear. I'm going to be great. And I adore you as well. Thank you so much, my love. For becoming the most devoted girlfriend imaginable."

"Thank you for a wonderful experience. And if you're having problems, if you're mad, and you're not sure what to do, call here. If it's an emergency, they'll come for me. You mean something to me." Diana had to leave after we embraced the more time. She grinned as she walked through the office to the grounds, and I turned around and returned home with a significant burden on my back.

I didn't listen to music on the drive home because I tried to find out how to confront my father without entering into a big argument or informing my mother that something bad was wrong. So I couldn't make out what was going on. I thought that if I could only fake it, I'd be able to get through it. I'd never been such a fine liar. I was about to discover the reality.

The trip, which was the only time I rode it that summer, flew by. As I arrived at 10:15 a.m., everybody was up and watching TV in the living room. Camilla came up to me and embraced me tightly as soon as I stepped in, which helped a lot. She had a slew of concerns about my time with Diana and Diana herself. I informed her I needed to say hello to mom (forgetting to mention dad) and that I'd be with her in a few minutes. I kissed mom on the cheek and nodded to dad as though he were a stranger. He wasn't exactly friendly with me either. That's fine with me. I sat down and addressed Cammy and my mother's concerns, but my father remained quiet. I figured mom and Cammy didn't realize the icy barrier that separated us. They'd get it eventually, but not tonight, I pleaded.

After a few comments, I said I was exhausted and used the restroom before going to bed. Fortunately, I was so exhausted that I fell asleep quickly, but it was a restless sleep.

XXXXXXXXXXXXXXXXXXXXXXXXXXXXXXXXXXXXXXXXXX
XXXXXXXXXXXXXXXXXXXXXXXXXXXXXXXXXXXXXXXXXX
XXXXXXXXXXXXXXXXXXXXXX

I returned to my work and home routines during the next few days, and I went out a few evenings with my friends or brought Camilla to dinner, a ball game, or a movie. Whatever it takes to get out of the bed. I called Diana on Thursday night and informed her that things with my father were still grim. She was sorry she couldn't be there for me, but I assured her nothing she could do.

My mother captured me on Friday night before I went out, after a few days of apparent coldness between my father and me. My father went to play poker (or so I hoped), while Camilla went to a friend's home. "Okay, Jon, your father isn't going to tell me what happened between the two of you. So tell me what you think. Why do you and your father resemble two icebergs? What in the world happened to you?" I stood there, afraid to tell her what I learned, but mom was a strong-willed woman who refused to let me past her.

"I'm not going to worry about it, Mum. I'm sorry, but I just cannot. He and I got into a heated argument. You just have to leave things at that."

"No, I don't. With this gulf between you, you're not going to school in five weeks. Then you and he hash it out tomorrow afternoon, or the four of us can talk it out on Sunday. Four, to be exact. Your sister as well. Do you believe she hasn't heard what's going on? She hasn't revealed something about you, has she?"

"No, not a single word. Yet I think I've found she's concerned. I'm just so worried...mom, I can't talk about it with you. Please allow me to speak with him tomorrow. I don't want to drag you or Cammy into this, and I particularly don't want to drag Cammy into it."

"That's fine. I'll leave it to you two to work it out. If you do, that's fantastic; you don't have to tell me about it. But if it's still an issue, we'll do it my way." She turned and went to the kitchen to do whatever it was doing, and I decided to remind her. I was dying to inform her. Yet, I couldn't hurt her heart in such away. I couldn't do it.

I went to work the next day, washed up when I got home, and my father came into my room while I was finishing up getting ready. "Jon, you and I are heading out to eat. It was the two of us." He seemed to be in pain, as though he was about to get his teeth polished. That's just how I thought about it. I said I'd see him in ten minutes.

We climbed into his car as mom drove Camilla away in hers. Dad and I hardly spoke as he went me to a casual steakhouse, nothing expensive, sort of like a discount restaurant with no other locations. We ordered a couple of drinks, perused the menu, and placed our orders with the waiter without mentioning each other. I don't say anything.

We sipped our drinks, trying not to think about the elephant in the building. I was now able to break the silence. "I know mom forced you to do it, but you called this conference. But let me see what you're thinking."

He squirmed in his seat as he hemmed and hawed. "We know why we're here, Jon. I thank you for not informing your mother of what happened the other day..."

"Please be patient. The only reason I've been silent is because of the harm it would do to both mom and Cammy. For the time being, how it affects you is the least of my worries."

"So, that's what there is to it? You don't want to know my side of the story?"

"What is your point of view, Dad? What might it be? I discovered you with another guy. How do you justify it because your mother permitted you to do so? Was it your first time with someone? What about her, whatever her name is?"

"Kelly is a girl. She works in my workplace. No, that wasn't the first time. What else would you want to know?" He was almost challenging me to ask him now; he seemed adamant.

"How much longer, Dad? How long would you be with...her? Is she the first to do so? And importantly, why? Why would you inflict such pain on your mother and risk losing your family? An order to..." I spoke in hushed tones, only above a whisper, "...a sliver of tail? Is that what there is to it?"

"Jon, there's a variety there. Do you want an answer? That's fine. It wasn't our first time. It's been going on for over a year. And she isn't the only one. She's the second in line. And, yeah, I suppose it's about sex. Your mother..."

"Wait a minute. If you're about to say something intimate or derogatory about mom, I'm not sure I want to hear it. Don't blame her for this. You are the one that is deceiving." The rest of my life seemed to be collapsing around me. My father has been cheating on me for a long time. And he was attempting to accuse my mother in every way. What was the identity of this stranger?

"That's fine. Let's just claim I'm in desperate search of something I can't find at home. Not like the manner I like. You have daily intercourse or did before the summer. You're aware of how things are. A guy has requirements." The waiter then came over with our dishes, and as he went, I looked down at my plate as if it were horse poop. I couldn't eat anything. My stomach was clenched in knots. And Dad was devouring it as though it were the finest steak in the country. "Are you not going to eat? And sure to request a to-go bin." It was as though nothing had happened. That's how I feel if you've ever seen the movie Invasion of the Body Snatchers, which is about people being substituted by seed pods. It was my father, but it wasn't my father. Despair washed through me.

"Dad, put the goddamn knife and fork down!" I nearly yelled. It was noisy enough that people at surrounding tables stopped eating and turned to look at us.

"Don't yell at me!" he snarled. "I'm still your dad!"

"Well, maybe not for long. I don't recognize you. I feel sick to my stomach like I'm sitting here with a stranger saying insane stuff. So, what do you think would come of this? Are you trying to stay with mom? Are you leaving? But for how this would affect Camilla, I think you should leave. You're not dedicated to your family."

"And so, you're leaving for school in a couple of weeks? Do you suppose we can all abandon your mother and sister at the same time?" That had me thinking. I'd have to sit at home if he went. Regardless of my father's financial contribution, I will not abandon them. I'd still miss Diana. We couldn't make things function over a long distance for years. Maybe a few months. "Besides, you're mistaken; I'm loyal to our family, which is why I'm staying."

"Then what's your solution? Live a double existence as I hold my mouth shut and grow to despise you? Won't you even suggest wanting to sort it out with mom? Because you're right: if you go, I have to stay. I won't leave them behind."

"Jon, the life I had with your mother has been gone for a long time now. You don't want to hear about it? Well, I understand. I do. So you can't expect me to give it up. I'm 42. Son, listen to me. Please." His demeanor shifted from stubborn and obstinate to begging for empathy, and I saw a sight of the father I had once known and cherished. I sighed, and he informed me what he wanted to know. "I know this is a difficult subject for you to hear from your father, but your mom...she gave up on sex years ago. No details, but we used to enjoy it, like most couples. Then it tapered, which is normal, but then it stopped, which isn't. She wouldn't go to talk about it, either on her own or as a couple. It's been a few years." He wasn't wrong, but I was also irritated and perplexed.

"Father, I'm sorry. I'm sorry that something...happened with mom. I think it's a horrible thing to deal with, so why not get a divorce and pass on?" "Dad, I'm sorry. I'm sorry that something...happened with mom. I imagine it's a painful thing to live with, so why not get a divorce and move on?"

"And I love your mother, even without sex, and I love you and your sister. Do you think it'll be easy for me when you leave for school? I'll be proud of you, I AM proud of you, and I'll miss you as much as your sister and your mother would if we can work things out. Look, I could never have brought Kelly into our home.

At the very least, I melted for him. I might appreciate his condition because I was in a relationship where sex was a big part. I was also upset over him sleeping with somebody behind my mother's back. But as a guy, I could relate.

"Are you sure you can't speak to mom? Won't she get help? It might be a medical issue."

"We won't find out, and she won't speak about it. Maybe it's time I questioned her more aggressively. I won't inform her I've been having intercourse, but I will tell her that's my next move. It's not 100% truthful, but it's more honest than I've been with her. Can you take your sister on Monday night, and I'll talk to her?"

"Well, I will do that. But you need to speak to her. Don't chance her finding out the way I did. It would ruin her." "I'll take Cammy to the Yankee game. We'll be away from 6 until around 11. Dad, thanks for being truthful with me. I'm always mad, but I can see things from your perspective to some extent." I wanted something to suck up the beer that I had consumed. And when Dad and I returned home, Mom noticed we were doing well. I was still keeping his secret, and as I looked at my mother, who was still a stunning woman at 43, my heart secretly went out to her. I couldn't speak to her about their dilemma (it was difficult enough talking about it with my father; I couldn't do it with my mother), but I thought they could.

I spoke with Diana on Sunday night, and we made arrangements for her day off, which was scheduled for the next Wednesday. It seems like a year away. Dad and I talked in my room before bed that night, making sure I was still bringing Cammy to the game the next night and that he was going to speak to mom. "I'll hold your secret as long as you do, dad, and I swear I'll never tell her as long as you try."

I was nervous all day at work on Monday. I requested to depart at 4 p.m. rather than 5 p.m., and Sy agreed. "Your mind isn't here today anyway; go, and come back tomorrow with a calm head," he said gently. He and Marilyn were nice bosses. It was difficult to work, but what career isn't? Before someone mentions Diana's work, I'll warn you that it was the most difficult of all. She was in charge of the welfare of 20 children. People value their children the most in life.

I went home and showered off the day's sweat, and when Camilla got home, she hopped in as well before putting on her Yankee tee and cap (her favorite player was Louisiana Lightning's Ron Guidry) and heading to Yankee Stadium. I purchased her dinner (hot dogs and Pepsi, of course), and we watched the Yankees defeat the Orioles 5-3.

Cammy asked me on the way home, as we were stuck in traffic in the Bronx, "Jon, what's up with mom and dad? Does it have anything to do with why you and dad were arguing last week?" Smart boy and perceptive. I looked at her and saw that instead of being sleepy, her eyes were bright and open. What might I tell her? I despised lying to her. However, not everyone was intended for her ears.

"Honey, I can tell you this: dad and I had a battle, over something I don't want to speak about; we're mostly over it, but even mom doesn't know what it was about, and she was able to let it go; so I'm going to ask you to do me a favor, as my sister that I love and admire, and let it go as well. Can you do that for dad and me?"

"I wish you wouldn't treat me like a little girl! I wish everyone would quit treating me like a kid! It makes me feel like you think I'm a boy!" She sat there pouting, and I felt bad for not telling her the facts. However, it was for her benefit. I didn't want to hurt her heart about something that was always bothering me.

"Camilla," I said, hoping it sounded adult, "I know people say this to you all the time, and believe me, they did the same to me when I was your age, but there are certain things you're not old enough to understand fully. There are always things I'm trying to understand. It's complicated. Life is complicated."

"I guess that's up to mom and dad, but if they inquire, I'll tell them they can invite her!"

Camilla slept for the remainder of the flight, but it was relatively silent. The poor thing was worn out when I arrived at the door, so I took her in. There was no arguing, which I felt was a positive thing. Mom was seated on the sofa, watching the television, while dad was in their study, the door locked. Mom seemed to have been weeping.

Cammy was sleeping with her arms around my waist. "Mom, are you okay?" I questioned as quietly as I could. "Would you like to talk?"

"Put your sister in her room, I'll come up and get her ready, and then I'll come down and speak to you; just wait up for me." I brought Cammy up to her room and went to my room to settle while mom had Cammy ready for bed.

We met back in the living room and, tired as I was, listened to mom as she poured her heart out to me. "I know your father told you things I wish he didn't share with you. But I'm glad you're back to talking to each other."

"Mom, I'm not sure how much I should relate to you about this; it's pretty awkward talking to you about anything so personal; listening to dad was difficult enough."

"I know. I'm not going to go through depth beyond what you know because learning, you know that stuff is humiliating enough for me as it is, but I want to ask you one favor. A huge favor."

"If I can, mom, I'll do it. You know I will."

"Your father and I need some time to work on our marriage together, alone. We want to go away for a week, the last full week in August, Sunday the 19th through Saturday the 26th. Then we'll all be home for about ten days before you have to be at school on Tuesday, September 4th. Would you stay around and look after Camilla? I know it's a lot to ask of you. You'd have to quit your job a week early to be around for her. But if you can...well, your father and I need this. We love each other, and we have to try to work this out."

I didn't have to consider it. "I'm delighted to assist you, Mom." Diana will also be at camp next week, her last week. So I'm going to make amends with Sy and Marilyn. They might be dissatisfied, but they must realize. I'll inform them that we need more family time before I go. It'll all work out. Overall, caring for Cammy isn't exactly a punishment for me. I'll ask Diana if I should bring her with me if I see her that week. If not, I can not attend. I'll do everything I can for you and your father, mom."

Mom was sobbing heavily and reached in to hold me tightly. "You and your girlfriend are the most wonderful things we've ever done." We raised two wonderful young people. So, your sister is on her way. She's very intelligent and mature. You are our pride and pleasure." We stayed nearby for another minute or two. "OK, Jon, thank you. You can go to bed now. Otherwise, you won't be able to wake up on time in the morning." She kissed my face, and we went to our rooms after turning off the lamps.

For the first time in a week, I lay back, feeling optimistic for my family. I'd go to whatever length to save their marriage. I'd even totally forgive my dad.

XXXXXXXXXXXXXXXXXXXXXXXXXXXXXXXXXXXXXXXXXXX
XXXXXXXXXXXXXXXXXXXXXXXXXXXXXXXXXXXXXXXXXXX
XXXXXXXXXXXXXXXXX

The next evening, we ate together as a family and told Camilla that the last week of August will be just her and me, that mom and dad were having a holiday together for the first time since I was born. She welcomed it gracefully, relishing the opportunity to be the object of my focus. Mom made arrangements for them to spend a week in Hilton Head that day. I informed Sy and Marilyn I wanted to leave a week early than expected due to family obligations, and although they weren't excited, they agreed. On my last day, they gave me my paycheck plus a cool bonus for the previous two years, as well as good luck at school money. As I previously said, they were wonderful people.

The following weeks went as expected, and things at home improved. Except for the first week of August, while Diana was with her family, I went to see her every week. I still went up with Cammy on Family Day. The remainder of the summer was perfect.

Whenever I went to see Diana by myself, we reserved a space at a hotel to be ourselves. We made love, had sex, and did whatever made us happy. We'd get food at a deli or pizzeria, eat at the park, and then return to space for more playtime. She also got permission for me to come in for the whole day last week when Camilla was with me and taking her with me. I had the impression I was being screened for a role the next year.

After lunch, we were lying on the bed one of those afternoons, me in my boxers and Diana in a pair of simple black panties. She didn't carry her sexier lingerie with her for the summer because wearing those panties in front of the girls and employees wasn't necessarily realistic. It didn't matter; I was only happy to spend time with her. What she wore had nothing to do with how beautiful I thought she was.

We were silent, our hands teasing and smiling with each other. We continued to kiss on and off, romantic and caring. Diana quietly replied, "I love you, my sexy Bear." Despite their tiny size, her breasts rose and fell with each breath, and just staring at her had an impact on me. She laughed when my hardon poked her thigh.

"I adore you, my beautiful Angel." Or do you want to be my naughty Devil?" I licked my fingers and gently rolled them all over her areolas, first the left, then the right. Diana relaxed and giggled as a result of my presence.

"Your Devil, without a doubt." Right now, I'm feeling especially naughty. So take advantage of my situation. "You should be my filthy Bear," Diana said as she wrapped her arms around my neck and kissed me the most that day. "Or my hunky stud lover." "Just come and get me." She knelt on the floor and backed away from me, teasing and manipulating me by tweaking her nipples with her fingertips. "Come on, big guy," I say.

"I'm on my way," I said enthusiastically as I pursued her on the bunk. Diana chuckled with delight and seduction as I caught her, and she practically pushed me on my back. She smiled widely before kissing and biting my cheek, then down my chest while her tongue licked from my right pec to my left, including my nipples.

"You're delicious, Bear. Savory. "Except your hair," Diana chuckled. "Can you please shave your chest the next time?" She said this with a sly grin on her face.

"Of course. Then I'll shave under my head, knees, and pubic hair. And we will apply lipstick to my lips and braid my hair." I was always busting her balls.

"Wow, Joanna, I think you'd look adorable!" We were all laughing hysterically and wrestling on the bunk.

I moaned as I pushed the crotch of her now damp panties away and assaulted her lips with my tongue and teeth, a fresh sensation that made me quake with her. Diana leaned back into my face, her big hips opening her anus.

I was captivated and wanted to give it a shot. I yanked my fingers out of her clutching pussy and put the tip of my first finger on her anus, applying only enough pressure to let Diana know what I was up to but not enough to enter her. I left it up to her to make the decision; I wouldn't do that if she didn't want me to.

"It's okay, Jon," she said clearly from down by my groin. Give it a shot. Just make it quick. And if I order you to quit, you best stop fucking now."

"You know me better than that, honey." Simply relax, and if you say no, that's the end of the matter." I pressed a bit more, and she groaned. I made sure to keep circling her clit in small circles with my other hand's fingers to keep her arousal up. I pulled gently, her natural juices and my saliva acting as lubricants for my finger. As I was in there,

"Are you well, Angel?" "Would you want me to stop?"

"NO! " Don't give in! Go a bit faster, and continue sucking my clit!" I could sense her hot breath on my wet balls, so I didn't press her to do something more than enjoy herself. My fingertips slipped in and out of her butt while I continued to tease her clit, and Diana had a series of orgasms as she fucked my fingers. Then she let out a huge scream, so loud that I cringed, afraid that somebody might call the cops. After a minute, Diana collapsed on my body, lifeless as a wet noodle. I gently retracted my fingertips from her orifices, and she only cried quietly.

"Are you well, Angel?" "Did I cause you pain?" I was licking the back of her head and caressing her leg.

"Of course not, stupid," she said quietly, still sobbing. "I mean, there was some discomfort at first. But then it went out, and there were so many feelings, and it was so beautiful the way you did it. I didn't think I'd be able to resist cumming." She turned over and grabbed my face between her embrace. Diana kissed me, not with an intense kiss, but with a long, sensual kiss full of love and affection. "Thank you for proposing it, and thank you even more for being so gentle about it."

"If that is what my Bear desires..." She lay next to me, whispering filthy stuff into my ear in a gentle, seductive accent. Her look looked far from angelic at the time, but it didn't matter. Her hand pumped me quickly, rubbing the glans with her lips, and I blew my load in bursts, covering her face right above her left eye to her jaw, and even some on her throat. Diana was a beautiful mess when I was finished with her. "What a sexy Bear."

"You're an incredible lover," I said, kissing Diana repeatedly as the shadows in the room became more orange and longer.

"Every day, every day." Angel, you lit a fire in my mind. I never imagined I could love someone as much as I love you."

"You're a talker. What you've done to me... "I never thought sex could be so much fun, so...HOT before we met, and I was taking control of my orgasms," she said with a light chuckle. I'm not sure how else to put it. I adore it when we are gentle and caring. I still do; it's so lovely. So I like it when we get down and dirty together. And what about Jon... I would never have guessed all of this might have occurred just a few months earlier. I had no clue what it was like to be in love. It's a thousand times more than I should have hoped for. It's because it's you, Bear. Bear, my lovely. "My adoring Bear."

We hung on as long as we could before getting into the bathroom to clean ourselves so we didn't stink of sex anywhere we go. We paused in a small town cafe for a light dinner before leaving (it was a hot, sticky night, not good for a big meal). As I dropped her off at camp before 9 a.m., we embraced, still hating this aspect of our day together, saying farewell. "Are you sure I can't entice you to come back home with me?" I made a joke.

"There are just two weeks left, Bear." We'll spend time together on and off for a week, and then we'll be at school together. "We'll be together so much that you'll get bored of me," she said softly.

"It would never happen. The day, though, would never arrive. Unless a swarm of cheerleaders in pompoms surrounds me."

"It's a male pig." She slapped my chest with the same fun with which I made the joke. "Maybe I'll have those huge sexy football stars to look after me!"

"Hey, if you can figure that out, do it!" We both burst out laughing. We were lighthearted and not at all serious. We were madly in lust with each other.

"Drive home cautiously, Jon," Diana cautioned as she stepped out of the vehicle. "Are you carrying Camilla next week?" "Are your parents leaving?"

"That's right. She had a wonderful time on Family Day. She's excited to see you as her counselor for the day. Sheryl has been very gracious to me this season."

"You can guarantee she's got a reason." She'd like to have you as a counselor for next season. It's for recruiting."

"I worked it out. Nonetheless, everybody here has been very friendly. I'll think about it if you come back next year. Assuming we're in the same space. I'm hoping so."

Diana was pressing in next to me. "I think so as well. Bear, I think we get to spend a long time together. It's been a long time." There was an unspoken thought there, something that must have frightened most 18-year-old boys. The prospect did not frighten me. I was thinking along the same lines. However, dreaming about it and learning about it are two very separate items.

"I'm the same way. So let's wait to see how the academic year goes. If all goes well, I'd like to do this again next year. I see how much you love it, and I think it's a great movie to take advantage of it while we still can." We kissed each other goodnight. "Angel, I adore you. Please call me on Thursday, and I'll see you on Wednesday."

"Bear, I adore you as well. I adore you." She moved back behind the office, and I went home by myself. Even though I had to tackle traffic for much of the way there, I loved the trip to see her in the morning. And with straight roads, I despised the drive home. Thank god the summer was coming to an end.

Cammy and I were left behind after our parents flew down to South Carolina the next week. If a crisis arose that I couldn't solve, our aunt Molly and uncle Maury were just a twenty-minute drive away. I wasn't concerned. I was confident we'd get along just fine until I had appendicitis or something. We've still done it.

And that's just how that week went. Cammy and I got along so well that I just had to "pull rank" a few times. We went to another Mets game, she stayed out with friends a few nights, and I had friends over another. On Wednesday, we went to see Diana, and Cammy spent the day with her squad while I was assigned to a boys group. Softball, a morning swim, brunch, tetherball, a music practice (with a ridiculously sexy music teacher), an afternoon swim, some socializing time, and finally dinner. What a long and boring day. I was singing around the campfire. And it was time to go. The only drawback was that I hardly saw Diana all day.

Cammy and I walked together to my vehicle, our arms around each other. "I was so preoccupied with those kids that I hardly had time to miss you," I explained. "I'm not sure whether that's nice or wrong."

"It's both. That is all I have every day. I love to miss you, but I don't get enough chances to do so. Until the end of the day, "Diana said quietly. "At that stage, I can't avoid thinking about you."

"I can't wait until you get home on Sunday. I'm going to do a variety of amusing stuff to you." Don't worry; Cammy was at least 50 feet away from my vehicle. "I wish I could kiss you like I want to. I've had my fingerprints all over you."

"You'll have to make do with your mouth on mine. And don't expect me to be available on Sunday night. I'll spend time with my family before retiring to my bed! There is no warning! If you call before 11 a.m., I'll destroy you!" We laughed and kissed a couple of times.

"Okay, so Monday, you're mine all day! And though we just lay on the sofa and watch TV all day."

"That sounds ideal right now. And one night," she said softly as we approached each other, her hands on my chest, "we have to try what we discussed last time."

"No way, not in my vehicle. That can happen while we're alone in our beds. We'll just have to wait before we get to classes."

"Come on, Jon, let's go!" Cammy phoned. "Don't you two kiss a lot?"

"It's never enough, Cammy," Diana said. "You'll find out someday!"

It was now time to go. Cammy also had her camp the next day, which was her last day. I didn't want her to miss it, so I had to get her around.

"We'll be together next week, Angel. I can hardly wait."

"Bear, neither do I. I'll call you when I get home on Sunday. It should range between three and four. Now, hurry up. Often, drive cautiously."

"Always and forever, my darling. I adore you."

"I adore you as well. Bear, you'll get there."

Cammy told me about her day on the way home and said she wanted to go to sleepaway camp next summer. She'd be able to be on staff in a couple of years. It was both thrilling and heartbreaking to see my sister grow up in this manner. In certain ways, I thought she could remain a child for a long time.

The remainder of the week flew by. Cammy had a happy and emotional last day at camp, and she cried a little as she got off the bus. I took her out for her usual Chinese meal, but she wasn't really hungry. She was well by Saturday, and we picked up our parents from the airport that night. They stepped off the plane with beautiful tans and huge smiles. Mom hugged Cammy, and I was hugged, my Dad. "How are things with you?" I asked quietly.

He grinned, his vast white teeth standing out against his tanned skin. "That's a lot easier. We thought about it, and...well, let's just hope things are starting to get a lot easier for us. Thank you, Jon. About something." He held me again, and I vowed that everything I learned would be kept safe in my head for the rest of my life. Then I embraced mom, who thanked me for taking care of Cammy. I was thrilled to see the content and at home.

Diana returned home the following day. I didn't see her, but we talked for over an hour on the phone, starting to make up for our summer apart. It was wonderful to realize that we could communicate anytime we liked for as long as we wanted. I, on the other hand, couldn't wait to see her.

Diana asked me a question at the end of our discussion "So, Bear, do you have some spare time throughout the day? Will and Walt will be out all day, and my parents will be at college." I could see she was up to no good.

"Cammy is heading to the pool club with her friend Dana now that my parents have returned to college. So I'm yours for the whole day."

"So, give me a few minutes to sleep, then give me some time to get up. Come over at 1 p.m.? And the door will be unlocked, so come on in." She giggled in a manner that drove me insane.

"I'll be there; you can bet on it. May I pack something to eat for lunch?"

"I have items in my home. Simply carry yourself. Even the libido!"

Diana's words sent my mind into overdrive. That night, I spent time with my dad, reading a book as they watched a bad movie. But I couldn't focus on the plot. My thoughts were on Diana and what she had planned for our day together. It sounded special. I was curious...

The next day, I arrived at her house at 1 p.m. and recalled simply let myself in. As I opened the gates, I saw a small sign on the wall by the stairs, about 20 feet away. It just said "up," with an arrow pointing upstairs.

"How are you?" Just in case, I called out. "Pay attention to the signs!" Diana called out from behind her closed door. Another sign at her door read, "Strip, then switch sign." Okay, I'd participate in her playing. It was a lot of fun. Except for my boxers, I changed out of my clothing. Then I flipped the sign over, and the other side said, "All!" I couldn't help but chuckle because she was so familiar with me. I removed my boxers, then a sheet of dark paper covering the rim. "Now come on in!"

As I entered her bedroom, the curtains were closed, so the room would have been very dark even throughout the day, except for the dozen or so candles that were lit. "MMMM, My handsome Bear has arrived, nude for me. A naked bear. "She chuckled, and I laughed along with her. Diana was on her back, dressed in a short silky purple robe wrapped around her waist and black stockings on her hips.

"Angel, welcome home. Those signs were adorable. You know everything there is to know about me."

"I do. Bear, my quiet friend. Or are you timid? Do you want to have some fun? Are you having the same sexy feelings as I am?"

"You'd be wise not to. My lover can exercise more self-control." Diana crossed her knees, and I almost passed out with desire. "Now, my darling, come here. Allow me to demonstrate how much I missed you."

I didn't require another invitation. I slipped into bed beside my lover and said, "Hello, sexy girl. You seem to be a one-of-a-kind gift for me."

"Gift packed," she exclaimed as we embraced passionately from the outset. I slid my hand inside her robe and felt nothing but skin from her tummy up, but she wore lace panties on the bottom. I thumbed her breasts one at a time as we embraced, and she moaned as our tongues danced together. "I've missed making you available anytime we wanted. And I need you right now. So many to tell. Too much to tell."

Diana said with a filthy smile, "I'm doing something naughty to you." "I haven't been able to wear something sexy this summer, and now that I can, I want to have a good time."

"Damn, Diana, that's awesome." Whatever I was looking for or planning before I arrived at her door, it wasn't that. "Hold still," I muttered, lost in bliss. "Leave the job to me." Diana let me fuck her thighs after she started shifting her legs. It looked silky smooth; every time I went all the way, my balls brushed against the nylon, bringing a dimension of gratification to what we were doing. What I was up to.

Diana drew her robe open to reveal her left breast and directed my mouth to her very hard nipple. I sucked greedily as if expecting milk to spill. She moaned alongside me as my hands continued to squeeze her cheeks and I began pounding my hips as hard as I could. My climax struck, and my scream was muffled by her beautiful breast, a soft little mound encircling a hard nub. My cum poured all over her breasts, the sheet, and even my fingertips and her cheeks. It was a heavy, hot load that momentarily exhausted me. I let go of her breast and moved my lips to hers, embracing her with all the love I had in my heart for her.

"That, Angel, was...indescribable. Nothing that I had hoped for."

"Perhaps this is why it was indescribable. And when you arrived, the sensation was...indescribable for me. "She said this with a sexy chuckle. We kissed so passionately, lovingly, and beautifully.

"Just one thing," I explained. "You didn't get to have fun doing it."

"Oh, my dear Bear, I disagree. It was a lot of fun for me. I get a kick out of seeing you proud. This summer might not have been the same without you. I am giving the long trip alone to see me nearly every week. I'm in love with the concert. I wish we could have seen more of each other, but that wasn't necessary. You turned the summer much happier than it was before. And now we've been together for weeks and months. Who knows how long it would take. And there will be more years. Even though we're young, I think about it."

"I consider that as well. I think we're both crazy, but it's a fun kind of insane. Our friends, on the other hand, will probably assume we're insane for even mentioning it."
"Without a question. But they have no idea what we're talking about. Or, for that matter, do, though I suppose they have a good idea. Or a deplorable notion." Diana leaned against my chest while I tickled her back and shoulders. We were about marriage...again. That wasn't the first time this had happened. Did we still value each other so much at the age of 18 to pledge to each other for the rest of our lives? We were all going to the same college in a week. Time will say, I reasoned. Just time will say.
XXXXXXXXXXXXXXXXXXXXXXXXXXXXXXXXXXXXXXXXXXX
XXXXXXXXXXXXXXXXXXXXXXXXXXXXXXXXXXXXXXXXXXX
XXXXXXXXXXXXXX

Diana and I spent the following week shopping for items we wanted to go away for months. And some of those months will be bitterly cold and snow-covered. When we weren't shopping, we hung out with my colleagues, who had become Diana's friends. We have spent time with our friends, both individually and together, including a night together. She came over for dinner at my house on Thursday, and I went to hers on Friday. We were also family-oriented individuals.

We couldn't have as much fun as we might have wanted because her cycle arrived during the week. We predicted it; after all, she was on the pill, and it's quite boring. Diana still tried to look after me throughout those weeks, but if she could do without, so could I. At college, we'd have plenty of time. We thought, at least.

Monday was our last day at college since it was Labor Day. Diana and I went to a party in the afternoon, but we agreed to meet our families at Marco's at 5:30 for an early dinner since we had an early start in the morning. Also, by being early, the tiny restaurant was willing to handle our reasonably large group of nine without having to wait. Diana and I stood together, and Cammy insisted on staying on the other side of me. She was going to miss me badly, maybe much worse than my parents. And I was going to miss her much more than I was going to miss my parents.

It was a nice and sad evening, made much more memorable for Diana and me because it was the location of our first date. Our families had been allies, and my parents had become happier than they had in a long time. Diana and I went to be alone about an hour after we left at a little after 7. We both agreed to be

173

home by 8:30 p.m. So we went to what we felt was 'our' place, a small clearing near the restaurant. There would be no fooling around. To be honest, just a bit. We simply desired to be isolated for a short period in a familiar and relaxing environment.

We stood in the center, arms around each other. We weren't losing each other; we were walking to school together, yet there was a sense of a significant difference in our lives. Can we make it? Will we be tempted by meeting too many different people?

Diana said, "You haven't sung to me in a long time, Bear. Please, would you sing something?" I considered it and chose a Simon and Garfunkle tune, 'April, Come She Can.' It's a short album, and it's sort of sad, so maybe it wasn't the right option. But it's a lovely tune, and I sang it well, even though I couldn't reach the high notes that Art Garfunkle did. Diana shed a tear at the conclusion. "Why did you pick that, Jon? You sang it wonderfully, but it wasn't what I was hoping."

"I'm not sure. I've always thought it was lovely to perform, but I can change it to something more suitable for us." I then sang 'America,' another S&G song with a slow, sweet sound of two young lovers exploring America. That was even more interesting, something relevant to our lives. We would begin the next chapter of our lives in the morning.

It was difficult to say goodnight, but we were all heading up to Binghamton together. Her parents in their car (minus Will and Walt, who were heading to a friend's house when they woke up to conserve space in the car), my parents in theirs, and Diana and Cammy in mine, a mini caravan of three cars full of clothing, music, and other stuff, including my stereo. We were scheduled to leave at 7 a.m. No, no.

"Jon, I adore you. That's my Bear. It's a positive thing we're moving there together. I'd be scared if I were to do this alone. I'm really afraid, even with you."

"You're not by yourself. It's frightening for me as well. But we'll make it through this together. And you'll be valedictorian this time. To first place!"

"HAH! I realize I'm clever, but Binghamton is full of them. I'll only be another face in the crowd."

"Hey, let me tell you a story. You'll never be a 'face in the crowd.' You would stick out because you are both amazingly gorgeous and extremely brilliant. Of every crowd, you stick out. And I'm very proud of you." I gave her a long and gentle embrace. "I've been proud of you."

"I'm proud of you as well. You're intelligent; you had to be to get into Binghamton. You're dDianastatingly attractive. "With a wide grin, she said. "You still have a wonderful singing voice. You should make use of it there. You may sing in a chorus, a song, or just for entertainment. Bear, I don't want to conceal it. It's beautiful."

I looked Diana in the eyes, those gentle blue eyes. I thought we could have stayed up late together. However, there was much too much to do in the morning. We said our goodbyes, and I arrived home just in time. I spent time with my family until 11 p.m. when we went to bed. I didn't sleep for long. I was curious whether Diana slept. I was curious about what it would be like to live apart from my home. I was perplexed by a plethora of issues. I was curious.

Tuesday at 6 a.m. was absurdly early, particularly given that you had only gotten around four hours of sleep the night before. That's roughly what I received the night before. Yet I awoke, fired up, and able to take on the universe. That's how I looked when my adrenaline ran out. I'd need a ton of caffeine at that stage. However, I was off to a strong start.

Before Camilla came in, I used the toilet, washing, showering, and putting my items in my shaving bag. Then I let Cammy in as I went downstairs to make a cup of coffee as our parents prepared.

Dad was the first to arrive, and he sent me a wistful grin and a hand on the back. "That's what there is to it, Jon. You're on the way to leave your imprint on the universe. You'll spend much more time there than you can here with us. Have you been extra sweet to your mother this morning? She cried for much of the night. We're happy for you and proud of you, but leaving home is always difficult for her." His eyes welled up as well.

"Isn't it difficult for you, too, dad? You are free to confess it to me."

"Okay, of course, it is. I'm going to miss you terribly." He embraced me tightly, and I hugged him back almost as tightly. "Okay, now for a couple of topics. Your money is in your bank account there, along with another thousand dollars from us.
Given that your room and board are covered, that should be plenty of revenue. However, if you need any additional information, please contact me. You're still aware of the importance of moderation when it comes to alcohol. At a band, it's all too tempting to get carried away and overdo it. I don't think I need to warn you about how to handle women. You're

already covered in that regard. I'm happy you've decided to go with Diana. Don't mess things up. She's a wonderful young lady. Take good care of her, and she will take good care of you. Study hard and attend school. And if you need us, you can reach us at any time. That's everything I can come up with. Oh, baby, we all love you very much." His expression was wet, cheerful, and sad all at the same time. I was weeping a little too.

"Dad, I'll be great, but thank you. I adore both of you."

Cammy walked in at the very moment. "Jon, I can't believe you're leaving. Who can I turn to for assistance?" She seemed to be in a bad mood at the time.

"I'm the same as I've always been. You'll have to do that over the internet. But, sis, I'll always find time for you. Only don't call me after exams or on Saturday nights, "I teased her, and she smiled instead of frowning. "After all, you don't have to say farewell for many hours. In my ride, it'll be you, me, and Diana. You have four hours to ask us something."

"Where's your mother already?" grumbled dad. "We have to reach the Glazers for breakfast at the diner in 20 minutes. Carol, what are you doing? Are you going with us, or will we leave you here? "He screamed as he ascended the stairs.

"Come on down!" Mom called out, and she arrived a few minutes later. "My boy is a college guy today!" she exclaimed as she kissed my face. It was mushy and awkward, and I adored her.

As I looked around, I felt so....melancholy, even though I understood why I was unhappy. I was happy to be returning, but I knew I would miss my home and relatives. More than I should have hoped for a week earlier. I double-checked that I had all of my school papers and everything else I needed to carry, and we were off, Cammy riding with me as we drove to the diner to meet Diana and her parents for breakfast.

They were already there, and I kissed Diana immediately as we all sat down to eat. Before breakfast, she and I placed our hands on top of the table, and then we all dug deep. Overall, we were a very silent party of seven.

We were on the road 45 minutes later, and the three of us were initially silent. Diana and I were still nervous, and Cammy was experiencing her own set of feelings. Not only were we close as brothers and sisters, but she had been close to Diana during the past six months as well. She was afraid she was going to lose all of us. But after a while, we started playing music and singing together, which helped lift our spirits and talked about all kinds of topics. It made me worry about how much I'd miss my younger sister. Despite our six-year age gap, we were both acquaintances and cousins.

I told Cammy in the last half hour of the drive, "Remember, we'll be back in a little more than a month for your Bat Mitzvah. We'll be before you know it. And, as I previously said, feel free to contact me at any time. If you need a girl's opinion, call Diana. We're both here to help you."

"Certainly, Cammy," Diana said. "Whenever you like. I hope I could be as loyal to my brothers as I am to you. As a result, you're never really isolated."

"What if you and Jon call it quits?" It was only natural for my sister to bring up a topic that Diana and I had never explored. Why will we do that? All was going swimmingly for us. We have no justification for thinking anything, but wonderful things were in store for us.

"That's not something we're going to discuss, Cammy," I replied. Diana and I adore each other, we get along seriously, and we have no reason to believe that something would go wrong. So don't think about it. Only know that all of us will be there for you." Cammy simply stood down. She was just a few hours out from saying goodbye to us. "Consider this: you have your toilet! There will be no more swapping!"

She grinned at the prospect of not needing to argue with me over the toilet. "That IS a perk. So I'll discuss it with you when you get home. Perhaps "She laughed. Looking at her in the rearview mirror, I stuck my tongue out at her.

Diana and I grabbed hands around the front seat as soon as we noticed the school signals. And the signs were leading us to our 'colleges,' as the dorm clusters are divided into. Diana and I were allocated to different dorms at Hinman, so we didn't know whether they were similar or far apart. I was assigned to Cleveland when she was assigned to Hughes, and it turned out that the buildings were just about 100 feet apart, entrance to entrance. We exchanged smiles. It was about as amazing as we should have thought.

Our three vehicles come to a halt in the parking lot between the two, and while our fathers remained with the cars, our mothers came with us to register for our room assignments and get keys. We had no trouble signing in for our rooms, and none of us was utilizing a huge sum of financial assistance (SUNY colleges were very cheap back in '79, we each had scholarship funds, and our parents made up the difference). According to what we heard, several students couldn't say the same.

We embraced for a minute...a mere minute...while making arrangements to meet for dinner at the dining hall, then went our different ways to move in. That's what I did for the next few hours—moving in my clothing and other possessions, including my stereo, posters, and other trinkets. I ran into Steve, my roommate, and his dad, and we supported each other with the heavy items. When I had gotten all of my belongings inside, it was time to say goodbye in the noise of hundreds of other people moving in.

Mom almost caused a scene, but dad warned her not to embarrass me. I said, "Don't be concerned, Dad. Mom gives me a huge hug." She did, with a few tears on her face that were quickly brushed away. Then there was another embrace (this time not as big) and a handshake from my father. And there was Cammy. I knelt to her level and embraced her. "If you don't act for mom and dad, I'll have to come home and hold you some more." She was the one who just didn't want to let me go. Still, she had no option, and I kissed her cheeks when my family left. Steve's left shortly after, and we began to get to know each other as we continued to unpack and set up our space the way we needed.

After I finished much of my setup, I went over to Diana's dorm to see how she was doing. I located her room easily enough (Hinman's buildings were almost the same style, so each dorm was identical) because, to put it frankly, her experience was not going well. When I passed by her room and tapped on her open door, I could see it on her forehead.

She sent me a glare as though she was planning a crime. "Jon, this is Robin," she said, pointing to her roommate, a lovely young lady. I extended my hand, and she shook it as if I were tainted. Oh no. Then Diana said, "Jon, I believe I left something in your vehicle." She offered me a glance that meant nothing was missing, but she wanted to speak to me.

We went downstairs and stood in front of the house. "They suggest you must wait a week before requesting a new bed. I could destroy her before then!"

"What's the problem? You said she's a devout Christian and won't be very agreeable in allowing us any alone time."

"That's just the beginning! As she discovered I was Jewish, she glanced at my head and wondered where I had my horns! The ancient, stupid anti-Semitic nonsense! My father got the shit while serving in the military during WWII! I'm not going to take the crap!" She jumped into my lap and sobbed a bit.

It's incredible that people really believed that bullshit in 1979. Diana made me feel worse. I wouldn't put up with the nonsense either. "Try to live with it for a few days, Angel. If she does something else like that, such as asking for your "tail" when she sees you nude, go to the RA (residence assistants) and see what can be said."

"Do you suppose I'm going to change in front of the psycho? There's no way! I'd rather do my business in front of YOUR roommate!"

"That's something I'd prefer you didn't do. At least not yet." We smiled, which relieved some of the stress. "Come over to my space and introduce yourself to Steve. He seems to be a decent person." So Diana accompanied me to my bed.

Steve was hanging posters as we came in. And there was a surprise for everybody. "What are you doing, Steve?" Diana exclaimed, her eyes huge and her voice high enough to knock him from the throne he was standing on.

"What about Diana? Diana, you're a jerk!" He jumped off the chair without incident, and they smiled and embraced like old buddies. That they were. Steve, a family acquaintance, was her one date about two years before we met. It's a little fucking country!

Diana went to introduce us after we exchanged pleasantries and inquiries regarding each other's families. "What's up, honey? We've already had a chance to meet."

"Of course!" says the speaker. They were joking, and I joined in, even though it sounded strange to me. They just had an old relationship between them, and just one meeting, but it was a strange situation. We all sat together, and I let them do the most of the chatting while they swapped tales. It took some time, but the three of us were soon getting along like old buddies. Their parents hadn't spoken much in the previous year, which is why Diana had no idea he was still in our class. After a lengthy conversation, we all headed to the nearest dining hall to see what dinner might be like.

It wasn't that terrible. There are meat, dairy, vegetarian options, sandwiches, puppies, pizza, cookies, soft drinks, and juices. It was very healthy. We stayed together, and it was obvious to me that they had no emotions other than friendship. Not that I didn't believe Diana, but it was a relief. Nonetheless, you never know.

After dinner, when darkness fell, news spread that a keg party would begin at 8 p.m. in the region between Hinman's six dorms. The RAs warned us to take it easy; orientation began the following day at 8 a.m. Of course, some people, being away from home for the first time, got stupidly wasted, vomiting in the restrooms.

Around 11 p.m., the group ended, and we all began to disperse to our separate quarters. Spending the night together was not an option, at least not that night, so Diana and I kissed and hugged in front of her dorm, drawing several snide remarks from passersby. That night, I'm sure there was some hooking up, just not with my wonderful girlfriend and me.

"I can't ask Robin to offer us rooms, and now I'll feel awkward that Steve even knows we're lovers, let alone telling him to give us privacy," Diana said before we parted ways.

"We'd best find out how to do one or the other, so giving up our sex lives isn't a choice. I love you, but abstinence for the next three months is just not going to happen!"

We both burst out laughing. "Don't worry; I'm not going to give it up either. Certainly not for you. I'm sure Steve would be fine about it, but it'll be weird for me. And I'm sure I'll have a new roommate within a few days."

As the evening chill set in, we clung to each other. Before we went to bed, I had an epiphany. "I didn't question you, honey. When Robin inquired about your horns, what did you say?"

"I told her I had a button on my ass that I pushed when I'm among gentiles to make them withdraw. I informed her that any

Jew had them. She was staring at me as though she wasn't sure if I was messing with her or not, so I offered to show her."

I broke out laughing in fits of hysteria, nearly collapsing on the deck. "Now you know why I'm not getting nude in front of her; she'll be looking for my ring!"

"The only button you have is between your legs," I smiled as I kissed her throat, ear, and mouth.

"Yes, you notice the one without any difficulty. Bear, we need to get some sleep. They're going to get us up early tomorrow." When I was already giggling, she kissed me. "He's a jerk. March on. I adore you, and I'll see you first thing in the morning."

As I went up to the bed and told Steve what Diana had told me, he burst out laughing as well, and I burst out laughing again. "She's such a jerk, isn't she?"

"Oh yeah," I said. "Brains, charm, and a sense of humor."

"Hello, Jon. I'm delighted for the two of you. You seem to be madly in sync with each other. Don't be concerned for me. It was a single date set up by our friends, and it didn't work out. I'll schedule a time for you and me to be alone here. Maybe we should figure something out so she can sleep over."

"Thank you, Steve. It will be fantastic. We'll discuss it until orientation." We kissed each other goodnight and relaxed into our new sheets, which cast new shadows on the walls and ceiling. Fresh surroundings. Fresh faces, new circumstances. It will take some getting used to.

We also had to reach our groups by 10 a.m. the following morning, which included getting up early to use the public showers and heading to the dining hall. Diana and I hadn't scheduled a time to meet for breakfast because our phones hadn't yet been linked, so I took a gamble that I'd run into her there at a quarter to nine. Steve and I went with a couple of guys from our hall (back then, the sexes were segregated by floor or corridor), but I didn't see her anywhere in the dining room when we got in line. As I was having my tray and silverware, I felt a hand grip my a$$ and almost fell as my new friends chuckled. She stood there with a huge smile on her lips. She was in a better frame of mind.

"Good day, Bear. "Good morning," she said, offering her lips for a kiss. I presented her to the guys in my room, and there was some fun ballbusting, such as asking her if she wanted to trade up if she needed spies to keep an eye on me, and so on.

"You're in a better mood today," I said as we allowed her to join us in line.

"That's right. Robin has already requested a separate bed. She didn't seem to like what I meant about a button on my ass. The RA said she'd see what she should do today or tomorrow. "Hopefully..."

"You're welcome, honey. I'm hoping your next roommate isn't fishing for your horns." We kissed briefly again before getting our tea, and she stayed with us like a Queen Bee.

"The timetable says we have a two-hour break for lunch," Steve said quietly. Why don't you and Diana get some lunch to go and enjoy some time alone in our room? I'm sure I'll find plenty to do."

"Hey, thanks a lot, kid. It will be fantastic."

"There's no issue. "Please let me know if there is something I can do to assist."

Until Diana and I parted ways to our orientation groups, I silently told her what Steve had suggested to me, and she gripped my hand and grinned. "Even though we just chat, we might benefit from some alone time."

"I'm sure we can do more than chat," Diana said, a knowing grin on her face. "We should carry lunch here, feed, and then you can owe me everything I've lacked so much."

"You're not the only one, lady," I said as we parted ways for the day.

The morning orientation session focused on getting to know the other men and women in the dorm. According to what I saw, if I hadn't had a girlfriend I adored above all else, it would have been a target-rich world. Several girls might have been options, ranging from normal to adorable to stunning. Still, in my opinion, no one should compete with Diana. On the other hand, Steve was scouting 'the talent,' as we used to claim. Maybe he did have a way about him, as he said to me during the summer. At the very least, he never had it with Diana. It must have been a difficult scenario.

During the two-hour pause, almost everybody went to the dining hall. It was our only meal choice before we began exploring the campus planned for after lunch in our groups.

Diana and I arrived at the dining hall quickly and requested sandwiches and fries. We brought them to my room and ate whilst discussing what we had learned in the morning. We had plenty of time after eating to do whatever we liked, and we wanted each other. We grinned at each other as we lay out on my bunk. We lightly touched and kissed each other, mocking each other and fanning the flames of our love. The light kisses turned into needing kisses in almost no time, and those turned into intensely romantic kisses.

"Angel, I need you out of your clothes right now!" I screamed in her ear.

"It'll be easier if we each take our shoes off. Bear, hurry up. I, too, need your assistance!"

We stripped as quickly as we had ever done before. "No, sweetheart," Diana said as I moved my head between her thighs. I want YOU to be inside of me. We may not have time for a second attempt. So come on in, and take your time. We must make this last." She wrapped her arms around me, and we embraced as though it were the first time.

We had to be vigilant when going about since the bed was a little bigger than the back seat of my vehicle but not as big as any of our beds at home. Spending evenings together might undoubtedly be entertaining, but that was a story for another day.

We kissed, sexy kisses that were not rushed. Diana turned onto her back, and I quickly found my spot between her lovely thighs, floating above her torso. She was at the bottom, but she was unquestionably the aggressor. "You said I could take my time, my little Devil. That's what I'm doing," I said, a wicked smile on my face and shaking limbs.

"My Bear is such a swindler!" "Are you sure you want to do that to me?" Diana inquired as she sunk her nails into my groin, causing me to moan with pleasure.

"Yes, Bear, so sweet," she exclaimed. "Take it easy and steady. Bear, my sexy."

We kissed with teasing tenderness, little kisses yet many, many kisses. We took things slowly and deliberately, making love with gentle and careful movements. She was swaying her hips underneath me, sending waves of joy across my core. My movements were doing the same thing to Diana based on the noises and gestures she was creating. Her nails rubbed my back, not in a harsh manner, just in the way that your boyfriend scratches your back when you have an itch. I was thinking to myself, "I wish we could do this every day."

Diana had a few soft climaxes while softly chewing her lower lip. "I want to be on top, Jon," she kissed me. "Turn us over."

"I'd love to," I said as I pushed her on top of me. Diana stood up instead of riding astride me on her legs. This was fresh to me, and I could see that we were connected even more easily. "Angel, you're so sweet!" Look down at our bodies as a whole!"

"Wow, that's hot!" We will have to do this in front of a mirror at some stage! Diana was so crazy and kink-minded, and I adored her for it. I adored her in every way.

She remained on her feet, jumping on my leg, my hands wandering her body, often soft, then rougher, sometimes fast, and Diana came twice, leaning down to kiss me to quiet her cries. We lay there, breathing heavily and softly sweating, kissing with passion. "I've been missing this the last few days," I said directly into her ear, making her laugh.

"It's only been three days, Bear...but I get what you're doing." It may seem like weeks at times. I wouldn't put my money on tonight. Did you know the phones would be used for on-campus calls? They're expected to be operational for full service by tomorrow, but they're still taking calls from all over campus. We may speak whenever we like. And those calls are completely secure."

"Maybe I'll make an inappropriate phone call tonight....to your roommate!" "Maybe it'll free her up!" Diana chuckled and slapped and kissed my chest. "Oh my god, we just have 20 minutes!" We both immediately sat up and noticed we had a crisis. We'd both stink of sex if we went back to our groups right then. So we didn't have time for a proper shower. I quickly instructed Diana to hold on for a minute. I put on a robe, went to the bathroom to get a big towel, wet it with warm water and a little soap, and brought it back to bed. We took turns using it to easily wash up and dry off with another towel. It wasn't perfect, so it'd have to do before we could wash later. Then we dressed quickly and dashed down to our groups with just a minute or two to spare.

"Did you have a good time?" Before our group began, Steve said something in hushed tones.

"I'm not going to share."

"Just assure my space isn't going to smell like sex." Getting a roommate, particularly one who knew Diana, was going to complicate things.

"I opened the doors," I mumbled. Then our operation began.

We got a full tour of the campus over the next few days, and some parties sometimes enabled Diana and me to be together and sometimes didn't. Our phones were switched on to all call home to tell our parents how much we enjoyed them and how good we were. We registered for classes, a slew of introductory topics, particularly for those of us who hadn't decided on a big field of research. Steve, Diana, and I went to the store for treats and such (he even had his vehicle, so we could take turns when we had the stuff to do together) and, of course, beer. The day before classes started, two wonderful things occurred: there were fantastic parties in each dorm complex as sophomores and upper-level students entered, and Diana switched quarters into my house. Not only did she wind up with a very cool sophomore roommate, but we were still only a short walk apart. It will be so better to be isolated from time to time.

We encountered Charlene, or Charli as she liked to be named, when helping Diana carry her belongings to her new space downstairs from us. Charli was a cute blond with medium-length hair and a beautiful grin, a bit bigger than Diana and a rounder figure. And, most of all, she and Steve clicked right away. It was wonderful for the four of us.

So the first week of school went well, except that the three of us freshmen had to adjust to the much heavier burden of homework and reading that came with attending a top-tier college. It took some adapting, but Diana and I had dinner together every night and breakfast and lunch if our schedules permitted. We ate at numerous fast dining establishments on campus that were included in the meal plan. But our other 'activities' had to be minimal before we worked out a good schedule, at least for the week. We intended to seek amends on the weekends.

That first Friday night, the four of us went out to a local bar with traditional bar food...you know, burgers, wings, salads, beer, and shots at a far lower price than downstate. Since Steve was driving, he stayed under his two-beer max, while the rest of us got a little tipsy, but nothing too bad. It was enjoyable, not dumb. As we returned to the dorm about midnight, we split up into pairs, with Steve and Charli returning to our space and Diana and I returning to hers. We had agreed that we wouldn't see each other until the morning.

We said hello to some of the unfamiliar faces in her hallway, some whose names she recognized and others to whom she just nodded and said hello. We both had several new faces to remember, many of whom we already met. That's how it is in a dorm.
We kissed and touched each other as soon as we entered her home, our hands running over each other's bodies. "Alone at

last," I whispered in her ear as I cradled her in my arms and raised her into the air.

"Yes, my stalwart Bear! We're alone for the night, and I think we'll be alone for a long time. We might also wash together in the morning."

"It will be fantastic. I'm not sure about sex in the tub and people going in and out."

"Cumming in and out," she laughed heartily. "That's one hell of a pun, Bear."

"I didn't think about it," I admitted as I removed her top and kissed the side of her mouth. Diana moaned as she unbuttoned my top and raked her fingertips through the hairs on my chest. All she did to me felt wonderful, and the fact that we could have privacy all night and into the morning without having to think about when we had to get home added to the experience. "Angel, I adore you. I'm thrilled to be here with you. As if destiny had forced us together so that we could share our lives."

"Bear, I adore you as well. I admire your ability to be romantic. But I like it when you get down and dirty with me. That's just what I'm looking for right now. My nefarious Bear. So seductive." Any comment was accompanied by a kiss somewhere on my face or body. "Take a seat in my office chair. Until I finish this." Diana immediately opened and removed my jeans, followed by my shorts. She removed her bra and shorts but kept her panties on, a slim black, lacy high cut pair. Her body was flushed, and she was beautifully beautiful. And with the dim light from her lamp by her bedside, I could see it. Diana was really attractive, but she first had to do something for me. What a wonderful girlfriend!

"Is it just lust? What about romantic love?" She had a playful and nice twinkle in her gaze.

"Honey, love is still there. Every day, week, and month, twenty-four hours a day. Someday it will be a year, and probably several more years after that."

The playful expression changed to a severe one, always laughing yet genuinely caring. "Jon, you're the sweetest guy I might ever hope to meet. When I envisioned my ideal guy, I never imagined him being nearly as nice as you." I continued to brush her face lightly, and she twisted her head and kissed my fingertips. "Allow me to do what I want to do with you now." I sunk lower in her chair, my legs farther apart, and Diana's tongue moved faster, only calming my glans and crown.

"My super Angel," I grumbled. "The greatest in the country, and oh so sensual." Diana had her lips involved, easing down around the head and eventually accepting my cock in her throat, and my legs swayed a bit. She had a unique quality about her. When she offered me a blowjob, it was never done only to appease me, as though it were a duty for her. She did so. She wanted to make me happy because she wanted to feel like she had more power over me. I could see how she felt;

Diana didn't say anything to me; instead, she kept bobbing her head up and down, teasing and enticing me with her tongue. My lower body moved in sync with her up and down movements. I leaned back, a low sigh escaping my throat, and my love went quicker. If I let myself go, it might have happened in a matter of minutes. Perhaps if it had been earlier in the evening, I might have allowed myself to cum, but the hour, the long week of studying, and the evening out with alcohol had me thinking this would be my only orgasm of the evening. So, hesitantly, I tapped Diana on the shoulder and said, "You'd best come to a halt, honey. This might be a one-and-done evening."

She was dissatisfied, but Diana knew. "So, what are we going to do, sweetheart? What do you intend to do for me...or to me? "She inquired, her face tense. The twinkle had returned.

"It's now your time to lay back and unwind a bit. I need something dripping hot. My throat is a little dry."

"Then it's a nice thing for you because I'm so wet," she said as I helped her to her feet, kissing her a couple of times before turning so Diana could sit as I pushed her scanty panties down. She stood and hurried forward, so her butt was on the chair's side. It was my turn on the field, and I supported her legs on my shoulders so she could sit at the edge of the seat comfortably. "Do an excellent job, sexy Bear. I'm horny, and I've been missing you too much." She traced her finger up and down across her lips, covering it with her warm honey.

"It's something I still do, isn't it?" I questioned as though I was offended. Yet I said it with a huge grin on my face. To demonstrate my claim, I took a long and slow lick from her anus to her clit. Diana expressed her approval by lifting her a$$ off the seat and letting out a loud moan.

"You do the strangest stuff to me, Bear." Diana was shaking her a$$ all over the seat while I teased her. Her back arched as she inhaled deeply, and her heels slapped into my upper back. After a few minutes, she shuddered during an orgasm that had her gasping, and before she could recover, I moved so that I could fuck her while still on my knees.

"My huge Bear, I adore you as well. You have such a wonderful feeling inside of me. You look great on me. I adore your body, and I adore the way you treat me!" Diana screamed as softly as she could as another orgasm jolted her.

She kissed me on the lips and said, "Without a doubt. You should unwind as I take care of you. Alternatively, we should take a seat on the bunk. Yet I have a suspicion the chair would be entertaining."

"Allow me to rest here, Angel. You are welcome to mount me." I paused for a moment and struggled to my feet before sitting (those tile floors will ruin your knees!). Diana shifted easily over my legs, straddling them. As were hers, my knees were separate, and I felt like I was farther inside her than ever.

Diana, it seems, thought the same way. "Oh my goodness, Bear! I can see you going further than I've ever felt before!" She was jumping on me fiercely, the chair legs were chattering on the tiles, and I was clinging to her for dear life.

She was holding me harder than normal, her muscles tense. We were groaning harder, so I drew her breasts to my lips to suck on her delicate pink nipples, and Diana came charging in, bringing my face up to hers to kiss me. Her tongue was probing about in my mouth, and her screams were muffled. I was lifting, my butt dangling from the seat as I gushed what looked like the largest load I'd ever come in my life. It was brilliant, beautiful, sexy, and caring all at the same time.

We were sticking to each other and were trapped as well. We were both as sticky as hell, also, with the space air conditioner, which was at best mediocre. When we were able to talk, I said, "Angel, you never fail to amaze me. Nobody might be a great match for me." I sent her a slew of gentle kisses.

"I'd say the same thing for you, Bear. Oh my Goodness, I don't think I'll be able to stay. My muscles are trembling." We gently kissed on the mouth, nose, shoulders, and sides.

"I'm hoping you'll be able to get up again. My legs feel a bit achy right now."

Diana laughed. "My tall, powerful man. He can't keep his petite girlfriend in place." She kissed me long and hard before standing up, our fluids already linking our genitals. With a sigh of relaxation, I rose from my bed. "Bear, I adore you. Thank you so much."

"Angel, I adore you as well. But you would never be needed to thank me. Not for loving you, but for having sexual relations with you. Not for almost everything."

Diana welcomed me, and I embraced her back. We needed to clean up before going to bed, so she handed me a huge bath mat, which I tied around my neck, and we went across the hall to the showers. I received a few whistles from the girls in the hallway, and I grinned, somewhat embarrassed. "Way to go, Diana!" one of the other girls exclaimed, while another said, "Hey, can I borrow him for the night?" before we got into the tub, around from the toilets. It was all in good fun, and I noticed that some women might be as mean as some boys. Since the coast was open, I peed in a stall until we re-entered the shower and washed each other a little faster than normal. We ran back to her space after brushing our teeth.

We were snuggled together in bed not just because we needed to but also because there wasn't much spare room for two adults. We couldn't lay on our sides, so we cuddled (I mean, sorry, poor me!). We chat about a variety of topics, mainly about adjusting to life with roommates and dorm mates. It isn't easy to adjust because you're used to making your bed at home.

We also were more at ease over the next few weeks. We observed Rosh Hashanah, the Jewish New Year, away from home for the first time. Still, since the school had a sizable Jewish community, they arranged a special dinner for every religious member who wished to participate. We developed strong learning routines, and Diana was on target for a straight A in the first semester. Steve and I both expected a B+ or A-. He and Charli transitioned from a romantic relationship to a more meaningful one, which made it far better for the four of us.

We (Diana and I) called home at least once a week, or our families did. I still had time to speak to Cammy, and once I called to chat with her, which delighted her even more, I placed Diana on the phone for her.

"So, are you excited for your Bat Mitzvah thesis? It's just two weeks away, "I informed her at the start of October. The ceremony was scheduled for Friday night, the 19th, with a dinner at a nearby catering hall on Saturday afternoon.

"Piece of cake," my confident little sister said casually, which made me chuckle. We spoke for a few minutes before she said something, "Jon, I miss you. I thought I would, but I didn't expect it to be this difficult to be without you."
When she said it, my heart ached a bit. "I miss you as well, kiddo. I'm preoccupied with schoolwork, I'm with Diana, and I'm meeting all these different people, so it may not be as difficult for me. Yet I do miss you terribly.
I'm looking forward to seeing you in two weeks. I wish I could linger longer and do something with you, but Diana and I have to return to school on Sunday. We'll be home Friday afternoon, maybe before you get home from classes."

"Jon, I can't wait to see you. I'm about as thrilled with it as I am about my Bat Mitzvah!"

She was adorable and friendly. "You know how to make me feel neglected, kiddo. We're ecstatic as well. Listen, we're going to see a movie, so I'll speak to you and your parents next week, okay? You do your best."

"You as well. I adore you, buddy."

"I adore you as well, sister."

XXXXXXXXXXXXXXXXXXXXXXXXXXXXXXXXXXXXXXXXXXXXX
XXXXXXXXXXXXXXXXXXXXXXXXXXXXXXXXXXXXXXXXXXXXX
XXXXXXXXXXXXXXXX

Cammy's Bat Mitzvah was a lot of fun. She was flawless the night of the service, saying her prayers and readings perfectly, and my parents were thrilled. I felt the same way. I was thrilled for her and my parents.

The following afternoon's party was a lot of fun, particularly for the honoree. Cammy enjoyed being the focus of attention, and she had a large group of peers, both girls, and boys, at the school. She danced with her parents, and several of the boys approached her. My sister was certainly maturing.

Diana and her parents were there, and she and I danced for the majority of the afternoon. I danced with Cammy a couple of times, once quick and once sluggish. She hardly touched my chest, but that was inches higher than she had been only six months ago. "You're growing up, baby. You're about the same height as Diana. You could be bigger than me one day!"

"You're correct!" Cammy laughed heartily. She was the happiest I'd ever seen her. "I'm delighted to have you here, Jon. I would have been devastated if you hadn't shown up."

"Do you think it's true that I wouldn't have come home for this, Cammy? I might have come even though I had to travel all night and day. My favorite sister is you."

"I'm your ONE and ONLY sister!"

"Oh, well, I forgot about that." When the song finished, we both smiled, and I kissed her on the face. After that, I went dancing with my mother while she danced with our father.

I kept her as though she were any other lady, just a little more distantly, with my right hand on her left and my left on her mid-back. "This is such a fun crowd, Mom. You and your father did an excellent job with Cammy."

"Thank you so much, Jon. I believe we did an excellent job both times. "She said this with a soft smile. "Isn't this a wonderful time? And your presence.... I've missed seeing you in the house. Your aunt as well, and don't even get me started on Camilla. She struggled too much when we returned home that night after we dropped you off. Just don't tell her I told you so."

"I'm not going to, Mum. She seems to be well right now."

"Yes, she is used to it, but we all miss you. And we're proud of you for getting off to such a good start."

"Thank you, Mum. It's good to be back home. Tell me how you're doing. Honestly."

"For the most part, I'm well. I'm a bit sore these days, so I'm fine for the time being. You and Diana seem to be in good spirits."

"It doesn't get much easier than this. We're having our assignments finished, and we're getting together about every day for a meal or two, as well as studying. We still take personal time where we should." Mom blushed slightly as I mentioned it, although I wasn't any more blunt with her than that. She got what I was doing. "You all realize how much I adore her, so mom...I'm madly in love with her. And she has the same feelings about me."

As we continued to dance, she smiled at me. "Jon, are you certain about this? Being in love is a profound and serious experience."

"Yes, Mom, I'm certain. And if we're all together next year, we'd like to move in together. Couples will stay at the kindergarten. It's a tiny apartment."

"So you want to share a house? I suppose I'm a bit old-fashioned in that regard, Jon. But if you want it by then, I won't object. Your father and I will continue to assist you as we do now. However, you and Diana will have to come up with something else you'll need."

"I understand, Mum. And thank you for everything you can do." As the song played on, we kept dancing, my mother and my first 'love.' There was one more question I had to ask her. "I was worried about that, Mom. I was dreaming of getting Diana a ring for Chanukah because of how we felt for each other."

Mom paused for a second as her brain caught up to her face. "Do you mean the kind of ring I'm picturing? Is it an engagement ring?" Her eyes were wide open, and she had a shocked expression on her lips.

"Yes, mother. I can't picture sharing my life with someone else like that. We've made a few hints about it. I'm 95 percent certain she'd say yes."

"Are you requesting permission or just informing me?"

"I suppose it's a bit of both. I'd like to think my parents would agree if I asked a woman I adore to marry me."

"Jon, you're very young. In chronological order. Yet you're a true guy in so many respects. Far wiser than your years. And she's a wonderful lady. If you still want this in a couple of months, Jon, I will owe you both my blessing in time for Chanukah. Your dad, I'm sure, will agree. Camilla, on the other hand, will be overjoyed. But be certain, boy. Make certain."

"I believe I am. The next two months will reveal more. Yet, I can't see myself feeling any differently. I'm madly in lust with her."

She held me tightly, and I was the one who was crying. "Jon, I adore you. You make me so happy."

"Mom, I adore you as well. Dad as well. Cammy, too...."

We kissed cheeks when the music finished, and then I went over to Diana and drew her back to the dance floor. She looked stunning in a navy cocktail gown, and I relished the opportunity to show the world how much I enjoyed dancing with her.

"Hello, lovely. Did you see I was dancing with other women?"

She sent me a friendly smile and said, "If you're wondering if I was envious, the answer is no. I wouldn't be jealous if you danced with a Playboy Bunny. Maybe a bit." As we swayed our hips and lifted our feet, she held me tightly. "So, would you like to tell me what you and your mother were discussing? You seemed solemn."

"I told her I met your ex-roommate Robin and that I'd been seeing her on the other. You know who I am, a true stud operation!"

"You are, after all, the sort. You're not going to tell me anything, are you?"

"No way. You could put me to sleep by torturing me. I'm not going to say anybody."

"Hmmm, I was planning to mess your brains out when we got back to school tomorrow, but now I guess I'll make you wait until after Thanksgiving," she teased.

"Who will be punished for that?" I replied with my sly grin.

"That is an excellent point. You'd have to be a fantastic lover, wouldn't you? Bear, my hunky, sexy guy. You are aware of my weakness."

"I do," I said as I embraced her on the dance floor. "I'm well aware of all your flaws, my lovely Angel. However, you have a couple of high points. The qualities that distinguish you as a remarkable woman. I adore you to the moon and beyond. I'll be doing this for the rest of my life."

Diana rubbed her face against my chest as we continued to dance. "Jon, I'm in love with you as well. Forever and ever."

XXXXXXXXXXXXXXXXXXXXXXXXXXXXXXXXXXXXXXXXXX
XXXXXXXXXXXXXXXXXXXXXXXXXXXXXXXXXXXXXXXXXX
XXXXXXXXXX

Midterms, celebrations, and Thanksgiving break are both on the horizon. Time whizzed past. The weather turned colder in Binghamton faster than it did elsewhere in the state. The first snows fell in early December, just as papers were being completed and finals preparations began. We'd also gotten used to college life and knew how to get our job finished. Diana had always decided she wanted to be a child psychologist, and she announced her major from the start. It was a more uncertain circumstance for me, but I had an open mind.

We were able to spend time together when we wanted to. Steve and Charli continued to see each other until Thanksgiving; they all preferred to have more fun than becoming serious with anyone permitted. Thankfully, they split amicably, and Diana and I could remain friends with both of them despite being dating other people.

Diana's family called my family to dinner as we went home for Thanksgiving. While we were away, our parents had been really sweet, and we had a wonderful time there with around 20 members of Diana's family. With two turkeys and all the sides, it was a crowded pair of benches. We were treated as though we were relatives. I understood just where my heart was.

My mom and dad both got the day off work the following day, so they brought me to the bank to their safety deposit vault. The bank assistant manager assisted us in retrieving the package before leaving us alone in a space that was almost too cramped for three individuals.

My father said, "Jon, I remember you told your mother you were almost ready to ask Diana to marry you. Are you confident you feel that way?"

"Yes, dad, I'm certain. We don't need to hurry to a wedding. However, I'd like to ask her. I thought it would be next month, for Chanukah. The only issue is that it begins on the 14th and concludes the day after school finishes. As a result, we'll be at school for the whole weekend."

"Yes, we are aware. But if you're certain, we're both thrilled for you. And we have something special for you." When he opened the crate, he discovered several jewelry boxes among the numerous documents, stocks, and other products—things my father gives my mother over the years and those they inherited from their mothers. A tiny square blue velvet box was included. Mom pulled it out and cracked it open. A stunning diamond was placed in a white gold setting, something antique and lovely.

For a brief second, I was unable to talk. This was obvious; I was being given a ring if I agreed to send it to Diana as an engagement ring. When I was first able to talk, I said, "That's lovely, Mom and Dad! What was the owner of this ring?"

Mom addressed me. "It belonged to your grandmother Sadie (her mother). She gave it to me not long before she died to pass it on to you or Cammy when the time comes. I always had your father's bell. We want you to have it if you want to offer it to Diana."

I was taken aback. This went far and above anything I might have afforded on my own. I had a couple of thousand dollars put aside as investments that I intended to use. "I'm at a loss for words. Cammy, how are you? I'm trying to be reasonable to her."

"First and foremost, your sister would have a young man to bring her a ring when the time arrives. We will assist him if he is a decent guy who cannot afford a bell. And there are several other things here for her, such as a pair of neckless', earrings, and other items that I carry now but want her to have. Some would even be for Diana, whether she is your mom. We're not going to choose favorites for the two of you."

I was quite taken aback. I took it in my hands, holding it by the ring section, and saw the light refract through the facets of the dazzling cut. Dad assured me it was a two-carat stone, and I was mistaken about the white gold. The setting was made of platinum. This was the kind of ring I couldn't even manage.

"I'm at a loss for words to express my gratitude. It's fantastic. It's amazing and extremely generous. I'm terrified to bring it to school with me and have it for three weeks."

"You're not going to," mom replied flatly. "It cannot be missed, nor do we believe you can. The twenty-first night of Chanukah is when you get home from work. I will be waiting for you when you get home. We'll also wrap it for you if you like. Then you should send it to her that night or the next day when it is still Chanukah if that's what you want to do. (Jewish holidays begin and finish at sundown.) You can't, though, bring it to school with you."

So we decided, and I kissed and embraced each of them. It was an incredibly gracious act that demonstrated how deeply they cared for Diana as well as how much they cherished me. Diana came to my house that night, and we just had a fun night with relatives, including time with Cammy. We had arrangements to take Cammy out to dinner the next night before I brought her home, and Diana decided to host her brothers as well. Not unexpectedly, they missed her as well.

We parked on the street a few blocks away from her home, my motor working for heat. Diana said as we stood silently in each other's arms, "What's going on, Bear? You've had a goofy smile on your face all night."

"I have no idea what you're talking about," I replied, a shite-eating smile on my face.

215

"You're up to no good. I assume you're not going to refute it."

"So, I'm going to refute it. After all, even though there was anything, you couldn't bring it out of me."

"Is that what you're thinking? Do you suppose I don't have other forms to get you to talk?" Diana inquired, her accent sexily lilting. She breathed gently into my ear, kissed my neck and ear, unzipped my sweater, and teased her nails down the front of my shirt. She was having a good laugh out of me.

"It's not acceptable! You're fighting in filth!" I sighed and cocked my head back.

"You're right. I'm going to irritate you, "She spoke breathlessly, igniting my fire with her incredible physical appeal. A single fingernail then traced up and down my now. "You're either going to tell me everything I want to hear, or I'm going to suggest you be a spy for our country because you're not going to break under pressure!"

"We're right here on the highway, Diana. The trees don't have enough leaves to provide us with shade."

"And you'd either be able to cum like this quickly, or you'd tell me what I want to hear."

"I'm not saying something. I have little to tell."

"Hey, it's not like my private bits are on show for everyone to see. If I have to, I'll hold you like this all night." This was developing into a very wacky game.

"So, go ahead and do that. I'll just sit back and let you offer me a fantastic handjob for as long as you want." I turned and caressed her soft boobs with my professional fingertips as I ran my hand up her top. Diana squirmed around next to me, breathing heavily, while I went under her bra and rotated her nipple left and right.

Her hand was pumping me harder and more firmly. Diana then opened my jeans all the way because she was now determined to make me orgasm, as though I were for her. "Thank you, Angel. Yours is doing your kind of magic on me." My balls were becoming closer and tighter, and I was grunting. As I placed pressure on her clit, her hips moved about.

We kissed passionately, our tongues gliding back and forth in each other's throats. What started as an investigation had evolved into a full-fledged exchange of emotion. "We'd best end, honey, before anyone calls the cops," I grumbled in her ear. We kissed again, intense, sweaty, passionate kisses as I exclaimed, "I'm going to cum!" Diana split our embrace with her mouth just in time to absorb my blasts of cum, swallowing me as quickly as I gave it to her. When she bent to suck me, my hand slid out of her jeans, so I softly pulled her up before slipping my hand back down her pants and rubbing her clit furiously. Diana was so heated at that point that it just took her two minutes to scream out her orgasm, gripping my hand and wrist with her thighs tightened.

We were still panting heavily as we tried to get ready before I brought Diana home for the night. We were fortunate enough that no one came out to check on us or called the cops on us. I got us out of there as soon as I was tucked up and my jeans were closed, not wanting to press our luck. As I was driving, Diana washed her hair and straightened her clothing as best she could. When we arrived at her door, we said a faster than normal goodnight.

"Are you not going to tell me what's going on?" She inquired once more.

"No, it does not. All I'll suggest is that it has everything to do with your Chanukah present. That's everything I've got right now."

Diana sent me a wide-eyed stare. "Bear, please accept my apologies. I should not have teased you in that way, and I should have simply let you keep your secret. I'm not sure why I acted that way."

"Angel, I'm not moaning. It was entertaining. I'm not sure what you felt I was withholding from you. Were you under the impression that I was dreaming about something else?"

"No, it does not. Ok, maybe. You had that ridiculous smile on your lips, as though you were dreaming about some lady. I was ridiculous, I remember. I'm aware of how much you adore me as much as I adore you. That is all my affection, my dear Bear." She held my face in her hands and kissed me as warmly as she had before. "Sometimes, I'm not sure what's wrong with me. I have the sweetest, most caring guy in the world, and I always feel nervous at times." She embraced me once more. "I'm madly in love with you."

"I'm in love with you as well. Don't be concerned. We do have our weak points. Don't you think I'm a bit envious when I see you chatting to a hot guy in one of your classes or even in the dorm? Yet I'm sure you won't cheat on me. As a result, I let it go. Diana, I know where your heart is."

She held me even softer this time. "Maybe you should even be a psychologist. You have a natural empathy for humanity. You often have a strong sense of self-awareness. Consider it. I can go until I don't go at all. We're bringing our kids out to dinner tomorrow night?"

"Yeah, ask your brothers and contact me in the morning."

We kissed once more. "Bear, I adore you."

"Angel, I adore you as well. I'll talk to you later."

The next day, we each did our own thing (Diana went shopping with her mother, while I went to Mike's for some time with old friends). Diana called to let me know that Will and Walt will be joining us for dinner. It was a pleasant evening for us, as well as a welcome break for both of our parents.

My phone rang when I was getting dressed, so I assumed Diana, Mike, or one of the other guys searched for a lift. "How are you?"

A brief delay. "Hello, Jon. How are you doing?" Adrienne was the one. I hadn't seen the voice since the beginning of the summer. She didn't attend Cammy's Bat Mitzvah when she was in California.

"Hello, Ade. How are things going for you? How is living in California treating you?"

"If you just want to know, California stinks. There are the phoniest individuals on the planet. It irritates me to no end! In the spring semester, I'll be transferring to Syracuse." For a brief moment, she sobbed. "I could not have gone. I despised it from the start. It's almost as though they talk a foreign language there! I really can't do it anymore." She was sobbing uncontrollably.

"Ade, please accept my heartfelt apologies. I really am. I'm happy you'll be close by. Binghamton isn't far from Syracuse. We will meet up on the weekends."

"What is Diana doing?" There was a sharpness about her that I hadn't seen since I last saw her at my graduation party. Was Diana right in her assessment that they were still bearing a grudge?

"She's fantastic. We spend a lot of time together. We have a great time there. We're going to have an off-campus apartment together next year." I didn't inform her about my Chanukah plans.

"That's fantastic," Ade said flatly, as though she had to pull a tone approaching excitement from her voice. Diana was on point that night at the club. They'd put up with each other for my sake, so they'd never be partners. At the very least, they were both attempting to help me.

We thought about life in general for a little while until Adrienne said, "Could you come up here this afternoon, Jon? I need to speak to somebody. A childhood acquaintance who really worries for me."

"Ade, I wish you had called sooner. This afternoon is well, but I have plans for the evening."

"Are you talking to Diana?" She almost spat out her tag.

"With Diana, of course. Camilla, as well as her brothers. Ade, I'm sorry you're hurting, but you have to understand that Diana, apart from my dad, is the most important aspect of my life. We're truly in lust, and I don't see that shifting anytime soon. I love you, you're my best mate, so if you can't live with this, if you can't be polite about her, you and I will have a major issue. We can't be buddies if you're going to be nasty whenever Diana comes up in conversation. Ade, I'd like to be your mate. But if you force me to choose...you're not going to be pleased with my decision."

Adrienne was nearly deaf. On the other end of the call, I could sense her anguish. I despised being in that role, and I despised doing things that were hurtful to her. "I adore you, Adrienne. And though we don't speak for months at a time, you've been my best friend for almost my whole life. I want you to be my best friend forever. If you had called yesterday or earlier today, I might have worked out a time to come see you."

"Please, Jon. And though it's just for a couple of hours." She was in pain. She was my best mate, for God's sake. I needed to carve out some time.

"Okay, I'll be there in an hour. But I have to quit by five o'clock. That adds up to three hours."

"Thank you so much, Jon. Thank you so much."

So I dialed Mike's number, apologized, and drove up to Westchester. She was standing by the entrance, and as soon as she let me in, she burst into tears in my arms. I hugged her tightly, allowing Ade to weep her heart out until there were no more tears to be shed.

She spilled her heart out to me for the next hour. How she despised the school, the people, and how her parents, especially her father, were furious at her for not even giving the school a full year. I'd known her parents my whole life, and her father, Marvin, could be a total jerk to her. It used to irritate me to no end.

I assured her that her parents would get over it in time and that they would also enjoy seeing her close by instead of almost 3,000 miles away. She and I would be willing to see each other, and even though she and Diana couldn't be colleagues, they'd learn to get along. She grinned, signaling that she was ready to give it a shot. It was the most I could have hoped for. She already had high school acquaintances from Syracuse and Binghamton, so she'd be around people she met and liked.

"Jon, thank you for coming. I'd be devastated if you weren't my mate." She hugged me tightly, which I returned. Her breasts were pressed against my stomach, her scent was reaching me, and I found myself physically reacting to a beautiful lady. I wanted to softly back backward, but Ade just gripped me tighter. She was kissing my cheek, then my neck, then my ear before I realized it.

I pressed back further, bringing us to arm's length. "Ade, I'm glad I could assist, and I'm glad to be your mate, but maybe we shouldn't sit too close together." My forehead was dripping with sweat, and my jeans were too small. Adrienne couldn't help but note what was going on.

"What's the deal, Jon? What are you scared of? Could you enjoy sex with anyone other than Diana? Do you think I'm stronger than Diana?" Her boobs were cupped in her lap, her red hair was wavy down below her neck, and she realized she was almost irresistible. Nearly.

"Greetings, Adrienne. I'm not sure what's wrong with you. I'm not sure why you can't understand that I'm loyal to somebody I adore and will never cheat on her. I believe we've reached the end of our friendship. You have little concern for me, Diana, or how I feel. When you called me earlier, I believe you intended to do this. And do not contact me again. "Never, ever."

Adrienne, enraged, yelled at me as I stood up and took my coat. "Get out there! You're probably a jerk anyway! What does that scumbag feel about fucking?"

I didn't take the bait. I had to say my last goodbyes to her family's home. I'd never go there. Worse, our parents' friendship will more likely suffer as a result of this. So I couldn't be concerned with it. Adrienne had transformed from a sweet and loving friend to a greedy, coveting, and bitter person. That day, I lost my second-best friend. Diana was, of course, my closest mate.

I was in a bad mood when I drove around. I always believed Adrienne had outgrown her....obsession? Whatever it was, it was always there, and our friendship was over. I informed my father what had happened when I got home, more than an hour before I had to pick up Diana and her siblings. He was depressed, as shown by his speech.

"Jon, your mother and I didn't want to say you this, but I would have alerted you if I had realized you were going there sooner. Adrienne is experiencing certain personal difficulties. Marvin revealed this to me at Camilla's Bat Mitzvah. Her behavior has been irregular for over a year, and she refuses to consult with a psychiatrist about it. He and Sandy are worried out of their minds. She said she'd be in Syracuse for school in January, but she's not. They're just going to pay for a nearby education, where she'll have to remain at home. I'm sorry you had to learn this the hard way." His sorrow had turned into a sort of desperation on his lips. Adrienne had been in his life since she was a kid, and he had seen her grow up. It was bad for him and his mother, but it was much worse for Adrienne and her friends. I felt dreadful.

"I wish I had known about this when you find out, Dad. I will never have went there today. Not with her parents at home. My concern is, what can I say to Diana? They don't get together, and I'm starting to realize why."

"You must inform her of the facts. It's still the right one. I wasn't truthful with your mother, and I did something I'll be embarrassed by for the rest of my life, not that I'll ever tell her. This because I couldn't be truthful with her about my emotions. Do not do this to Diana, particularly if you want to marry her. Don't begin your life together with a lie. Diana, on the other hand, strikes me as a very understanding soul. If she is aware of Adrienne's difficulties, she might be more understanding."

"Yes, she wishes to work as a child psychologist. I believe you are right. If she understands the whole thing, she'll sympathize. I wish I understood what I was supposed to do with Ade. I can't stay around here if she continues to want to come on to me, whatever the reason is. Yet I can't leave her if she's in too much danger."

Dad placed his hand on my back and squeezed it sympathetically. "If I had all the answers, son, I'd flee to God. I believe you'll have to allow her some time to calm down. Then see how you can contact her and speak with her. And what about Jon? Please pray for her." He embraced me, and I hugged him again. Despite the summer dilemma, my father was a decent man in most respects.

When it was time for us to go, I changed, and Cammy dashed down the stairs. My'minor' "Sister was no longer a kid. She was now 5'2" tall "She was maturing and blossoming, and she was turning into a true beauty. In a few years, God helps my parents.

We picked up Diana, Walt, and Will and went to a local Italian restaurant renowned for its hero sandwiches (subs or hoagies for those unfamiliar with the term). It was a lot of fun; the twins were already 16 and as big as I was, and Camilla had a thing for them. After dinner, we went to an arcade, which had pinball and video games, and I discovered Diana was an expert at pinball. It was simply a wonderful experience for everybody.

After that, I dropped Diana and her brothers off. We needed to be on the path by ten o'clock the next morning to get back to school by two o'clock, so it had to be an early night. Diana and I said goodnight in a rather gentle way for us as her brothers went inside, and Cammy watched from the car.

"Bear, you're thinking about something. I will tell you more about it all night."

"Yes, indeed. You know something about me. We'll meet tomorrow in the cab. It's nothing to be concerned with, Angel. As a result, don't let it hold you up at night." I kissed her deeply, just not too passionately. After all, my sister was watching. "Wait till we return tomorrow. I'm going to punch you for hours on end. Or at the very least one hour. It all depends on our roommates."

"Big fellow, I'm counting on it. I'm in desperate search of my sexy Bear. Despairingly." We laughed for a while, kissed again, and then it was time to leave.

Cammy said to me when I got back in, "Jon, you should have kissed her better than that. I must have turned down." She had a wide-eyed, ball-busting grin on her lips. "I remember what it's like to make out."

"Oh? Where did you practice how to make out? Or do I want to find out?"

"I've tried my hand at Spin the Bottle. You should realize that I'm not a kid."

"No, you aren't. I suppose I'll have to get used to the thought of you growing up. Just not too soon, please. And if you have any concerns that you can't ask mom for, please call Diana or me. We'll assist you. You're all about BOYS, right?"

Cammy chuckled loudly, but she still took my free hand in hers and squeezed it tightly. "Thank you, Jon. You're the greatest there is. I adore you."

"I adore you as well, kiddo."

XXXXXXXXXXXXXXXXXXXXXXXXXXXXXXXXXXXXXXXXXXXXX
XXXXXXXXXXXXXXXXXXXXXXXXXXXXXXXXXXXXXXXXXXXXX
XXXXXX

Another farewell with my family the next day, a few cries, but we were getting used to the breakup. I'd be out in a month for four weeks. We'd celebrate Chanukah a little late.

I was on time to pick up Diana, and as we drove down the highway, Diana asked me, "So, sweetheart, you want to tell me what was on your mind last night?"

"Let's learn about it. I didn't make it to Mike's yesterday. Adrienne called me, and she was distraught. She told me she despises California, that she dislikes going to school there, that she doesn't get along with her friends, and so on. I listened and spoke with her, and I felt she was getting stronger. She embraced me, then began kissing my face, throat, and even my ear, and I became aroused. This is purely a bodily response. When I attempted to drive her further, she became agitated and then furious. When I quit, she mentioned some truly heinous stuff.

So when I got home, I told my father, and he told me that Adrienne had been having major emotional issues for over a year. She told me she's going to Syracuse for school in January, but her parents won't let her go somewhere else than a commuter school. She refuses to accept she has an issue and refuses to get treatment."

Diana snatched my right fist with her own. "I'm so sorry, Jon. Honestly. I don't like her, but I know she's valuable to you, so she must be important to me. Besides, her behavior makes better sense now because she isn't entirely blamed for it. I'm hoping she receives some assistance. When she feels stronger, I'd love to get to know her for who she is."

I gently squeezed her back, but with deep love. "Thank you for your patience. You already realize that I don't want someone else in my life or my bed ever again. Angel, I'm madly in love with you."

"Never, ever? That is a long period."

"Do you suppose you'd want to be with someone else because forever is a very, very long time?" She made me feel a bit uneasy.

"No way, Bear. I'm not interested in anything else. I never look at other men that way. I'm very proud of you for standing up to Adrienne like that. She's a stunning lady."

"Angel, she isn't similar to you in terms of appearance. You're the most stunning lady I've ever known or seen. At least in my opinion."

Diana shifted her weight in her seat so she could smile at me. "You're serious, aren't you? I don't think so, Jon. I suppose I'm attractive. It's not bad. But I'm not particularly attractive."

"This is not what you can tell for yourself. I don't worry if you're short or if you don't have huge tits. I think you're stunning in every way. That includes inside you. Particularly what's on the inside of you. You're the most stunning lady I've ever seen, both inside and out. I adore the inside more than anybody else on the planet."

"What do you mean, bear?"

"Are you sure, Angel?"

"Please don't attack me when we get back. And make love to me. Slow and tasty. The way you do it very good. Bear, my hunky, sexy guy. We just need to get some food before we return. Since I'm not going to get you out of bed before dinnertime."

The remainder of the trip was spent humming to tapes and listening to the radio, with a lot of sexual excitement in the air. We wanted each other desperately. We stopped for a fast bite at a highway rest stop, and when we arrived at school, Diana said, "Hurry down to mine after you've placed your bags in your bed. Charli will not return from Buffalo until tomorrow. Surprising!" She kissed me in the vestibule, and I dashed to my room to unpack my bags and coat.

I arrived at her space a few minutes later, and Diana welcomed me and guided me straight to her bed. We were engaged in a deep embrace before we even lay down, and it continued as we climbed into bed together. We took our time undressing each other as though we were revealing our bodies to each other for the first time. I kissed her neck and chest, and she gently hugged my cheek. She was gently directing my lips in the direction she desired. Her jumper was off, followed by her bra, and her nipples were erect and urging me to pay attention to them. I licked my way down her shallow cleavage, tummy to her belly button, then back up to her light areolas and nipples. I swallowed one while fiddling with the other with my fingertips, then reversed, sucking one while pinching the other. Diana was whimpering and grinding her groin into my shoulder. We were still both wearing our socks, but my free hand tightly grasped her butt.

Diana was preoccupied with licking the top of my head through my briefs. That made me whine, which meant I was buzzing whatever nipple was in my mouth. "Oh, my sexy Bear," she growled, her voice blazing with fire. I unbuttoned her jeans with one hand and worked for my hand down through her underwear, which I could tell were lightweight, almost gauze-like, as I moved her on her back. I quit sucking her boobs and pulled myself up on my knees, leaning over her and staring her in the eyes. Diana had a dreamy expression on her face as she rubbed her palms on my stomach. We also realized what was going to happen next.

We took off our socks, then threw our underwear on the concrete. We kissed passionately. It was too easy to move in, but she was cozy when we combined forces. She drew my face back down to hers, and we kissed all over again, huge kisses, small pecks, and all in between. I went up and down, made some loops, and then returned to in and out. Diana reappeared, her thighs squeezing around my waist.

We didn't say anything. Instead, we made sexy sounds. Even though it was a bitterly cold day outdoors, our bodies were drenched in sweat. My hips rotated harder as we moved on, and my thrusts were more urgent. Diana gripped my arms as my hips brushed up against hers, and the bed protested our now heated fucking movements. Since I couldn't take it any longer, I kissed her passionately. We were panting heavily from the exertion of wonderful, passionate romantic intercourse. There was no conversation. We didn't have to do it to show our respect for each other.

I rolled onto my side, and Diana followed suit so that we were facing each other. She kissed my cheek and murmured, "You're incredible. As a lover and as a lover's passion."

"Angel, you, too. You get the best out of me. Even the beast is involved as well."

We laughed as we gently explored each other's bodies, our fingertips trailing lazily across each other's bodies. We drew the blanket around our bodies and squeezed as tight as we could, exchanging brief kisses. I wished I had the ring with me at the time. I would have proposed to Diana right there and there.

I borrowed her robe to go to the toilet, which hardly fit around me, and protected my lower parts even less. Diana chuckled at the most absurd thing she had ever seen as I tried to tie it closed, her 6'1" frame "boyfriend with wide shoulders in her little purple satin robe. I felt silly, so I didn't want to put on anything more than my panties.

"Oh, Bear, the robe belongs to YOU! You can hold it and wear it in front of the guys while you're on your floor!" She was giggling uncontrollably at my plight. "You're heading out there like that? Most of the girls recognize you. They will be able to see evidence that you are Jewish." There was another explosion of laughter.

"I'm only lightly protected. You're making me feel self-conscious, and I just need to pee!" I shook off the robe and put on my trousers and shirt while doing the Bursting Bladder Dance. Diana started giggling, so I dashed out to the toilet.

With a big sigh of relief, I relieved my aching bladder and returned to Diana's bed. She must have gone to the toilet when I was gone, so I stripped naked and returned to her bed, posing with one leg out straight and the other bent at the knee for her amusement. "See anything you want, lady?" I said when the door opened.

Charlie stood there, a wide smile on her lips. "If you weren't heading out with my roommate, sure. Do you suppose she'll let you have her for an hour or two?" I nearly jumped off the bunk, three feet in the air, when I hurriedly wrapped the blanket around me, my face three shades of crimson.

"Ummmmmm, hi Charli," I mumbled. "We, uh, weren't expecting you to return until today."

"Without a doubt. Now I understand why Diana is still so cheerful."

That was so humiliating. Charlie was smiling as she put her suitcase on her bunk, and Diana came in after we told her what had happened. The three of us then burst out laughing at what should have been an awkward moment. "So my boyfriend was flaunting his assets? Sorry, Charli, he's all" Diana grinned as she leaned on the edge of her bunk, rubbing my thigh under the cover. Then she told Charli, "We will get out of your way if you give us a few minutes. We can either go up to Jon's room or go to the common room and offer you some rooms."

"No, you are not required to do so. I'm the one who arrived early: the weather in Buffalo (where she lived) will be bad tonight, so I returned early. But what if I clear out and we go to dinner at 6 p.m.?"

That's why I spoke up. "No worries, Charli; we're not throwing you out of your bed. If you like, we should hang out. I'll dash upstairs, take a short shower, and put some albums down for us to listen to before dinnertime." Diana accepted, and Charli was relieved not to have to quit. So I went to my space (Steve wouldn't be back until late), took a shower and changed clothing, got a couple of Dead albums, and the three of us hung out, smoking a weed Charli had while singing along to a bootleg Grateful Dead concert song. We were starving by dinnertime (the munchies!) and had dinner together, a very big dinner. Charli was wonderful company; Diana and I both won the roommate sweepstakes.

Since we were both too occupied researching and finishing term papers, the last few weeks of our first semester flew by. Diana had to work harder than she was used to, and I was straining to keep up. Chanukah began on Friday the 14th, and there was a massive celebration that night, as well as a massive snowstorm that lasted all day Friday and through Saturday morning. The party was a mix of a Chanukah dinner hosted by the Hillel community (a Jewish students organization that Diana, Steve, and I entered in the spring) and a last major blast before finals the next week.

Diana and I traded small presents for the first seven nights; some were jokes, such as a pair of bunny socks I purchased for her, while some were more practical and still a joke (she bought me a pack of new disposable razors so I could keep clean shaved

238

for when I went down on her). We mostly studied hard and took exams beginning the next Monday, and by the time the exams were over on Thursday, everybody was mentally exhausted.

That night, there was a massive drinking party going on all over campus. But for a few overseas students who couldn't fly for various purposes, everybody checked out the next day to go home for a month. After a couple of drinks with mates, Steve left with his new casual lady, and Diana and I spent the night having a bad time together.

Diana began by watching her strip for me as some mellow George Benson played in the background, performing a little sexy dance while her clothes were spread around the bed. I was seated in my desk chair, staring at her as though it were the first time I'd seen her nude. She eventually wore just a pair of peach lace underwear, my choice of her hundreds of pairs. She enjoyed wearing sexy panties almost as much as I did.

She placed her hands on my back, kissed me on the mouth with the enticing tip of her tongue, and whispered in my ear, "Tonight, we're going to do something cool. Anything we've discussed, my sexy Bear." I shivered slightly at the thought; I knew just what she was talking about.

"Is that true? Are you prepared, Angel?"

"Yes, I am. We've been debating it for a long time." My hands moved slowly and deliberately across her body, gently flicking her thick nipples. They were so bloated that I could see the holes where her milk would eventually fall from. I drew her to me and licked her right nipple lazily, sending a small jolt of fire through her body. I did the same for her left one before standing up and putting her in the chair, only in her underwear.

"Now it's your turn to watch for a bit," I said as Mr. Benson's genius jazz guitar and voice provided a perfect groove to dance to. My top was easy to remove, as was my belt.

My love, I stood in front of her.

"Don't be so tender with me," Diana gurgled as I pressed my head against her lips. "I want to be gross tonight," she said before swallowing me again.

Okay. "Would you want to be my filthy little Devil?" I questioned brusquely, yanking on her fur.

When she struggled to swallow, my toes curled, causing my hips to twist and my balls to roll on her chin. As good as it looked, I had to put a stop to it, or I'd be pumping semen down her throat just too fast. "Don't feel too cozy," I warned her as I dragged her off the chair and onto the bunk. "Get down to your feet!" Diana was more than happy to comply when I told her what I wanted. Her body shook as I dashed behind her and buried my face between her cheeks to lick all over her anus. Diana let out a deep, low moan that could almost be heard in the lobby despite the rowdy party going outside.

"Oh, fucking crap, fucking shit, fucking shit, fucking shit, fucking Take my a$$! You can do anything you want to me!" Diana screamed as much as she could. When my thumb touched her clit, she covered her face in my pillow and gasped. Diana dropped over onto the mattress after her second orgasm ended, and I was on top of her, kissing her neck. "You're a really wicked child," she exclaimed exasperatedly.

"You're almost as bad as you are, Devil Woman." She jumped a bit when I gently slapped her behind. Then, in a much gentler tone that was more like mine, I said, "Are you certain you want to try anal? You are not required to."

"We've been dreaming about it for a couple of months already, sweetheart. At the very least, I'd like to give it a shot. You had me all sticky there. Let's get started. If you don't mind using some Vaseline, I had some in my bag." When her butt became slicker, I steadily moved a finger through her sphincter and her ass. Diana whimpered as she wrapped her fingers around my penetrating finger.

"There's just one way to find out," she exclaimed. "Put another finger in there then, and then spread me back."

Diana howled into the pillow as I attached my middle finger to the first one. I was sure I was inflicting pain on her, so I began to take my fingers out. "No, sweetheart, don't leave! This is what I'd like to see! Please, please!" Diana placed her free hand between her thighs and rubbed herself more vigorously while I kissed her shoulder and licked her neck.

"I'm not going to resist, honey; I'm going to end up popping all over your ass...outside!" Given how sweaty we were, we both laughed, so we both had a little more lube, and the time was right. "That's fine, boy. You're feeling strained. Tell me if it hurts so bad, and I'll quit, I swear. I don't want to inflict so much pain on you."

"I understand, Bear. It's now or never." She was on her feet, her bottom in the breeze, with her face on the cushion sideways. I got down on my knees behind her and pulled her legs further apart, lowering her bottom for me.

I pressed the head against her anus, drew in my breath, and pulled, causing the head to pop in the past her ring. "How's it going, Angel? So far, so good?"

"Yessssssssssssssssssssssssssssssssssssssssss "Keep moving," I slipped in a little harder, the Vaseline making things smoother despite her ass's firm grasp.

I hugged her cheeks, keeping a tight grip on her sensitive butt as I moved in slowly and steadily. I took a step back, then moved a bit further. Fuck, I wished she didn't interrupt me; it felt great. "Are you ready for the rest, honey?"

"That's all of it," I grumbled, unable to remain still before Diana arrived.

"That's so....fucking fine, Jon! Fuck me right here! And don't stop touching my clit!"

She was so close I figured she'd snap it off at the root. In, out, a little more Vaseline, and in and out again. We were both grunting like beasts, lustful, desperate animals.

Diana appeared unexpectedly, her body trembling all over and her face hidden in the pillow. That was the last straw for me as I emptied my balls deep inside her vagina, combining my cum with the lubricant, resulting in a very messy mixture. But none of us minded because we were engrossed in the wake of a novel, exciting, yet surprisingly personal encounter. I kissed her back and neck as my hands caressed her upper body, gently and tenderly touching her. The afterglow was as enticing as the climax.

"Angel, you know how much I adore you. How are you doing? Do you want anything?"

Diana, my Guardian Angel, said, "All I want is right here. I have the most incredible guy in the world who makes any encounter, sexual and otherwise, wonderful—every single moment. Don't budge. Don't leave the house. Only continue to catch and touch me as you have. That's what I'm looking for."

I drew her in tighter until her back was snug against my stomach. Her hair was in my face, and the fragrance of her perfume warmed me from the inside out. It was a perfume that will still remind me of Diana. "Angel, I adore you very much. More than anything else on the planet. As well as my family...though they are vastly different." We smiled as I kissed the back of her head.

Before heading to bed, we had to wake up and tidy up. We were happy staying together (just sleeping!) at that stage if Steve went back to sleep. It's what you get used to when you live in a dorm. He hadn't returned yet. However, he will come at some stage. In the meantime, Diana and I snored in my room. We'd be back to our normal lives the next night, so if anything went as planned on Saturday, it'd be better to spend nights together at home....hopefully. I was certain Diana would say yes, but I was always hesitant to approach her. I can't believe any guy doesn't have reservations or second thoughts until proposing to the lady he loves.

It's Friday, which means it's time to go home for the holidays. All was packing and saying their last farewells. We made arrangements to meet up with Steve, who lived about a half-hour away on Long Island during the holiday. We said goodbye to Charli, but it wasn't goodbye; we'd see her in a little more than a month, but she and Diana had grown close.

We were in a good mood when we drove along. We'd be spending a lot of time together during the next month, alone, with relatives, and with friends. Sy and Marilyn had called my parents and informed them that I could work part-time and earn some money if I desired. Why not, I reasoned. Whatever I earned will cover my living costs when we were at home, even though I worked part-time. I'd have loads of time on my hands.

When we got home at about 4 p.m., I assisted Diana in bringing her bags into her home. No one was home yet, but her brothers will be soon, so I called my mom at work and let her know we were home and that I was hanging out with Diana before her parents arrived, at which point I'd be home. We simply sat on the sofa, cuddled tight in the silent house, and relished the intimacy. I'm not sure why it seemed so special; we'd spent a lot of time together in the previous four months. It did, however, sound strange. And I realized I had something special in store for her the next day. So, when her mother arrived home, after her siblings, I said my goodnights to everyone and dragged myself to my bed, where my family was waiting. Hugs and kisses were exchanged all over. You don't know how much you've missed the great individuals in your life until you see them again.

We illuminated the last night's Chanukah candles and exchanged presents after a large dinner of my mother's brisket. I'm not sure what I got my parents, but I got Cammy a sterling silver necklace with a Jewish crown. She adored it, and I received the longest embrace of my life (or so it seemed).

"Jon, I've missed you too much. Thank you very much, it's lovely!" She was sobbing and unable to let go of my neck.

"Cammy, I missed you as well. I suppose I can't refer to you as squirt or kiddo anymore, can I?"

"I don't mind. I'm just glad to get you back for a spell!"

As she let go, I checked in with my mother to make sure the ring was in the house and packed for Diana. We then sat down and spoke to Cammy.

Dad informed her that I had something to say to her, and I sat next to my sister, my second favorite woman after my mother. "Cammy, you remember Diana and I are in love, don't you? We're not only in love with each other; we're madly in love with each other."

"I'm not sure what the distinction is, Jon."
"I'm sure you don't. It will be at least a couple of years before you fall in love. Not like me, your parents, or one of your colleagues. And falling in love is something much more strong. You consider sharing your life with the other guy. And that's where Diana and I are. We want to move in together in September of next year. And I'm going to ask her to marry me, to be my mom, tomorrow."
Cammy was taken aback at first, but then she burst out laughing. "Are you serious, Jon?" "Are you going to marry Diana?"

"If she says yes," I suggest. And I'm almost certain she can. We've discussed it, and I promise I can't picture being with someone else."

"I'm hoping she does!" She'll be my sister, well, sister-in-law. "Isn't that the same thing?"

"Sure, because of how you care for each other. Walt and Would will be like brothers to me. "We'll all be like relatives."

"When are you going to get married?" "Would I be a bridesmaid?" she inquired, her voice brimming with excitement.

"It is Diana's responsibility to choose her bridesmaids. But I believe it is quite possible. When would that happen? Not for a few years. We're not in a hurry."

She embraced me once more, all delighted and thrilled. "Now, Diana is coming over tomorrow to share presents with me. She realizes it would be a good present, but she has no idea it is a bracelet. So, please, don't say or do something that would warn her. Stay in here with mom and dad, and I'll accompany her down to the basement or up to my place, and if she says yes, you'll see her and the ring afterward. But there was no expression, no suggestion, no smile to reveal the surprise. "All right?"

"All right. "I'll be fine!" That was sufficient for me. I was tired at this point, so I went upstairs and fell asleep in minutes, although it was 9:30 p.m.

My mom woke me up at 10 a.m. the next day, Saturday, the last day of Chanukah, more than 12 hours after I went to bed. I stood up and returned to my old bathroom. I peed, shaved, then showered, and did some shaving. Overall, I needed to look my best.

I put on some stonewashed denim and an expensive medium blue jumper because it would be a chilly day. I ate a late breakfast whilst discussing finals and articles with my family and how I felt I did. I was optimistic, almost certain that I would end up with an A- average (3.8-3.9). Diana was confident she'd get an A. We should both be on the honor list. Working hard pays off.

I called the print shop and met with Marilyn, who was delighted to bring me part-time after Christmas to take a few days off. Then, at 1 p.m., Diana arrived with her family for a post-holiday get-together for coffee and pastries, as well as the exchanging of presents for 'the men.'

Her parents gave me and Cammy presents, while my parents brought Diana and the twins gifts. I had some items for the boys, and her parents had some things for Cammy. It was then time for Diana and me to be quiet for a bit. My family was aware of what was to come, but Diana's family was unaware.

We went upstairs to my place, and I shut the door. It was fine; there was no way we were going to have sex with a house full of people in the afternoon. We sat on my bunk, holding hands and exchanging warm kisses. "How did you sleep last night?" I inquired of her.

Diana gave a big grin. "Like a log!" says the narrator. I was exhausted, and my bed was extremely cozy! The only thing that could have made things more enjoyable would have been for you to be there holding me...and me to be holding you. Yet I was so exhausted that I must have just gone to bed."

"It's the same here. By 9:30, I was exhausted and in bed. Before I forget, tonight is a huge party at Poet's Corner. "It was our first date." I embraced her, and we both grinned at the recollection of our first kiss. My grin widened slightly; there was a certain symmetry to the group held in that specific club that night. "How is that?" What exactly did you bring me? "First and foremost, I!" I said it jokingly.

"All right, down there, kid!" "I assumed the ladies would go first."

"Yes, they do. "You're going to give me my gift first," I joked.

"All right, here it is. "Merry Chanukah, Bear!" She presented me with a large bundle in a neatly packaged case. I ripped off the wrapper to reveal a package from a nice men's shop (long out of business now). Inside was a lovely black leather jacket, lined on the inside and made of very smooth leather, almost buttery in feel. It wouldn't be warm enough on a bitterly cold night, but it would see a lot of use throughout the winter. And it was stunning.

"How is that?" "Say something," Diana said nervously, as though I didn't enjoy something too lovely.

"Dear Honey, It's stunning. Honestly. It's fantastic. Thank you incredibly much! "I adore you!" I clutched her close, hugging her body and shaking us back and forth. "I'm serious, Angel. It's the most stunning coat I've ever seen."

We kissed each other for about a minute until I let her go. "Your turn, let's see; I seemed to be disinterested about what I was doing. I was having fun with her. As she expressed annoyance, I patted my pocket and said, "Oh, that's correct! It's always been here." I took out the case, which was covered in costly textured white paper with a red bow.

Diana gave it an anxious glance. She was expecting jewelry, but I don't believe she was expecting a diamond. Certainly not the sort of ring she had been keeping secret from her. When she took the package from me, her hand trembling. "What did you do, Jon?"

"You'll have to crack it open to find out, Angel." I attempted to maintain a casual demeanor, but my stomach was churning with fear. She might, after all, say no.

Her fingers fumbled as she attempted to unwrap the tiny package while holding the paper and bow neatly. Diana then saw the blue velvet package and replied, "Do I want to open this?"

"I'm hoping so. It's a unique present for you." She exclaimed when she flipped open the package and saw the brilliant stone glittering in the lamplight.

"Oh my goodness, Bear. Oh my goodness!" Diana glanced at me, her upper lip quivering as though she was about to weep.

"Diana, my Angel," I began as I knelt on one knee, "I think when you meet the person you feel you belong with for the rest of your life, you quit searching." Why should I be interested in seeing who else is out there? No other woman may compete with you, let alone outperform you, not for me. Please marry me, and I pledge to love and care about you at all times for the rest of our lives. Whatever life throws at us, positive or poor, we'll face it together." She was sobbing uncontrollably at that time, tears running down her cheeks. I was worried that I had made a horrible error because she still hadn't taken the ring out of the package.

Diana sniffed out her tears, but her eyes were moist and smudged her mascara. "Will you place it on my finger if I say yes?" She was attempting to joke through her tears.

"Of course not!" Simply say yes first."

"In that case, Indeed!" Oh my goodness, Jon! Yes, yes, yes, yes, yes, yes, yes, yes, yes, yes, yes, yes Her hand shook as I clumsily placed the ring on her finger. It might have been a little smaller, but her hand looked fantastic with the ring on it, and they were both dainty and feminine. "Bear, I can't believe it!" I anticipated it someday, and I expected it fast, but you somehow shocked me! "I adore you to the moon and back!" She shouted as she drew me to my feet and smothered me with kisses.

"I adore you as well, Angel, forever and ever!" I clutched her as though I wasn't going to let her go. Still, I let her go with a couple more kisses and cries before we went back downstairs to share the wonderful news.

My family, of course, was aware of what was to come and were becoming impatient, asking why it was taking so long. But as soon as they noticed our smiles, they grinned back, and Diana, leading by her hand with the bracelet, showed it off to her relatives, telling them what was going on with hardly a word said. Her parents were wide-eyed, and they had no idea, but as the novelty went off, there were kisses, embraces, and handshakes all over. And Walt and Will, who still pretended to be uninterested, were delighted, and they warmly embraced and kissed their sister and shook my side. My parents pulled out two bottles of champagne to toast us because they knew ahead of time. Cammy and the twins were given very small champagne to toast with, little more than a couple of sips.

Diana couldn't stop crying, particularly when her father was making his toast. "To my lovely and brilliant daughter and her equally lovely and brilliant fiance." That was the first time one of us used the term about the other. It seemed great to me. "May you live a long and prosperous life with many happy moments to rejoice, and may the dark days be rare and far between." We all realize you're going to do amazing things in the universe because you can do something together. Welcome to our party, Jon, and we are delighted that Diana has joined Jon's family. And we can all be one huge happy family!" Cammy was giggling next to me as we both sipped our beverages.

"This tickles my nose, Jon," she said quietly. "It even tastes sour."

There was already some in her drink, so I took it from her quietly. "That's all I've got for you, kiddo. "Would you like some water or juice?"

"No, Jon, I'm fine." And she proceeded to speak over me to Diana. "Would you want me to be a bridesmaid?" I shut my eyes. The tiny amount of champagne gave my sister a buzz.

"You'd better be," Diana said with a smile. Cammy, you're like a little sister to me as well. "I wouldn't leave my sister out of my bridal group." Cammy bent over me and embraced her new sister as she always did.

"Does that mean we're going to be ushers?" Walt (I could now tell them apart....usually) questioned. They were both beaming with delight.

"I'm hoping so. What if your sister questioned her new sister, but I didn't question my new brothers?" They smiled at each other, as twins sometimes do, sharing some message between them. They then extended their hand and shook mine.

According to my father, "Nobody schedules anything for tomorrow night. We're all heading out to eat somewhere cool. Dream on where you like to travel, Jon and Diana. After all, it's your group." Diana and I stared at each other and decided just where we needed to go; we didn't need to talk about it. This is our place. It's Marco's. To talk without saying, you don't have to be twins.

Diana said this when we were alone again, in my car on the way to the Poet's Corner party "Bear, where did you find this incredible ring? It seems to be very ancient and very beautiful."

"It belonged to my grandma Sadie, my mother's mother. When I told my parents I wanted to propose to you, they gave me this ring. I couldn't refuse. It's just as lovely as you....almost."

She smiled at me. "Is this an old ring, Jon? Is this made of platinum?"

"Yes, it is, on both counts."

"Oh my God, Jon, I can't do it! It's much too costly, and it also belongs in your family."

"Angel, you ARE a member of my kin. You'll be there if I step on the bottle. My parents desired that you get it. I had no idea before the day after Thanksgiving when they revealed it to me."

"How long have you been worrying about this? Is it what you were trying to keep from me that night? You scumbag! You ARE capable of keeping a secret! If you can join the CIA. "With a grin, she said. "But seriously, Bear, I don't need this kind of ring. We should aim for something a little less extravagant."

"Okay, tell my parents you don't want this bracelet. I'm not going to. They want you to have it, to be a member of our family as much as I am. My parents want another kid. Angel, the ring is free. I'd like you to have it. With time, I'll have more chances to buy you stuff. However, this is a family connection. You're a member of my family, and I'm a member of yours. Angel, you will be remembered forever."

"I'm at a loss for words, Bear. I adore your relatives as much as I adore mine. They've made me feel like I'm a part of everything."

"The same way your family treats me. That is how it should be between all of us. And you brightened Cammy's day by inviting her to be a bridesmaid. She adores you as though you were her sister."

"And Walt and Will are delighted to be ushers as well. They've always taken to you, even though they don't reveal off as well as they can." We kept silent until we were a few blocks away from the pub. "Do you have the blanket in the trunk, Bear?"

As I looked at her, I saw passion and lust in her mind. I wished she saw the same in mine. "Yes, I have it on hand. Diana, it's quite cold outside."

"I believe we will be able to stay warm. I would like to make love to my fiance. That's a great expression, fiance. This is about all of us."

"My darling, I feel the same way. I adore you the most." I took a left at the next block and proceeded in the opposite direction, towards our unique clearing. We might have gotten a decent hotel space, but there was something unique about heading back to where we began our sexual awareness of each other, considering the cold and the car.

Of course, there were no other vehicles there on a cold winter night. On that very special night, we will be fully alone to make love. I left the car to keep Diana warm as I went to get my...our...blanket from the trunk. We were embracing ardently as soon as I got back there with her, a loving love surrounding us.

Diana was softly riding me, rising and dropping gentle and steady, and we were joining in blissful love within a few minutes. That night, that very special night, was one of the most entertaining and erotic encounters we'd ever had. We were all aware of it. We weren't doing something out of the ordinary. We were toasting to our passion for one another.

Our combined desire and passion kept peaking as we made gentle and sensual noises, as our fingertips searched out each other's bodies and kissed each other in the most beautiful ways. Diana had a few brief, intense climaxes that I could sense, radiating from the glans of my penis and expanding across my whole body. It took all of my effort to avoid cumming too fast. We needed this to be as long-lasting as possible.

"My Angel, you are stunning. I will stare at you loving me like this all day and night. Wow, I adore it when you hug me like that. You have excellent leverage of the body." I was rubbing her stomach, legs, and breasts.

"For the time being. You'll get me pregnant a lot of times, and after a few kids, I'll be all loose and obese, and you'll no longer respect my body. But for the time being, you're perfectly happy with my anatomy." Diana's hands traced the contours of my chest and shoulders.

"I don't worry whether your body shifts or not, Angel. You'll always be stunning in my eyes. What counts to me is what is in your heart. That is one of the reasons I adore you."

We kissed gently, our limbs moving in unison. As our motions were more frantic, our fingers joined together. "You promise, my lovely Bear?"

"What promise, Angel?"

"Promise to love me forever? For all eternity?"

"Without a doubt. My darling, I will always love you. Otherwise, I would not have asked you to marry me. So, how are you?" We were conversing while exchanging brief grunts of enjoyment. "Are you going to marry me for the rest of your life?"

"Oh well. We'll see what happens. Perhaps I can leave my choices open for the next twenty years." I gently spanked her bottom as she chuckled lustfully.

"That's for considering leaving me in twenty years."

"Maybe if you keep doing that to me, I'll change my mind."

Diana sensed it and leaned over to kiss me as well to get a proper perspective for her climax. We huddled under the covers, each of us radiant on the inside from more than just our orgasms.

Diana gripped me tightly. "You do realize I was kidding you before, Bear?"

"What do you think of replacing me in twenty years? Yeah, it was pretty clear you were crushing my balls."

"I sincerely hope not. I want to use those for the remainder of our lives. Whether that's okay with you."

"I won't mind, Angel. You have certain pieces that I'd like to use as well. For an extremely long period." We wanted to keep moving and dressed the best we could, even though it meant getting out of the car for a few minutes despite the ice. I carefully folded my new coat and placed it back on, comfortable and fluffy, before getting back in the vehicle. We kissed a couple more times before I drove away from the clearing and into Diana's place.

"You know, I always have to bring you that Chanukah present," I said, and she stared at me as if I was crazy.

"What are you on about? This ring...you would never have to buy me anything else!"

"I'll keep that in mind for your February birthday. Seriously, I did not purchase the bracelet. I invested next to zero on you, and you bought me this lovely jacket."

"Bear, I don't care how much or how little you invested. You still spent a lot of money on me. Besides, this isn't a competition. Keep your cash. I have no need or necessity for something else. I have your affection."

Diana took my right hand while I grinned and extended my right hand. "That is everything you will have. Why don't I treat you out for an enjoyable New Year's Eve dinner? We'll get suited up and go out to do something expensive."

"Hmmm....you've got a good bargain! That sounds interesting!" It was decided upon. A posh New Year's Eve. This is the start of several times we'll spend together.

We kissed for a long time at her front entrance, considering the chilly night. We had an amazing day and a wonderful night, and we just wished it could continue longer. We had to call it a night after a long time. We'd see each other the following day and almost every day after our Christmas vacation. However, it was always difficult to say goodnight.

Diana's nose was kissed first, followed by her lips. "Thank you, my Angel, for making me happier than I could have imagined."

"Are you serious? You're the one that made my day the best I've ever seen. That is, before our wedding. In that case, do you have any ideas about when?" We were also kissing each other on the mouth.

"I don't know. Angel, you will do most of the preparation. Isn't it what people dream of when they're girls? Only let me know where I should go and when I should arrive. "I made a joke.

"I believe it's a bit more complex than that. Let us sit down with our parents after the New Year to discuss matters. So I'm not concerned. We are not in a hurry."

As it turned out, that wasn't quite right.

Lightning Source UK Ltd.
Milton Keynes UK
UKHW020634010621
384730UK00011B/432